D1540506

Bob
It's been such a joy
to have shared an experience
as leader fans & enthusiasts.

9/17/05

Objects of Desire

THE ART OF FREDERICK CARDER

THE ALAN AND SUSAN SHOVERS COLLECTION OF STEUBEN GLASS

Objects of Desire

THE ART OF FREDERICK CARDER

THE ALAN AND SUSAN SHOVERS COLLECTION OF STEUBEN GLASS

Text and Photographs by Alan Shovers

Published by
The Evansville Museum of Arts, History & Science
Evansville, Indiana

This book is published in conjunction with the September 4 – November 27, 2005 exhibition of the same title presented at the Evansville Museum of Arts, History & Science and made possible by a most generous grant from the

Dr. William C. H. Grimm, Jr. and Phyllis R. Grimm Charitable Trust

Copyright © 2005 The Evansville Museum of Arts, History & Science
All rights reserved.

No part of this book may be reproduced or transmitted in any form or by any means, electronic or mechanical, including photocopying, recording, or by any information storage and retrieval system without permission in writing from the publisher.

Published by the Evansville Museum of Arts, History & Science
411 S.E. Riverside Drive
Evansville, Indiana 47713-1098
Phone: (812) 425-2406
Fax: (812) 421-7509
www.emuseum.org

Text and photography by Alan Shovers

Design by Semisans, Inc., Evansville, Indiana
Printed by Image Graphics, Inc., Paducah, Kentucky

Cover: Steuben Gold Aurene Jack-in-the-Pulpit Vase, Shape #751, 10 3/4 Inches High bearing print stamp signature of "Haviland".

ISBN 0-9709872-3-4

DEDICATION

1966 - 2005

To Edward, our son, who didn't live to see this day. With love.

ACKNOWLEDGMENTS

No doubt, my Carder Steuben "collection" would have remained a "collection of one" after my purchase of my first Gold Aurene bowl at the Del Mar, California Antique Show in 1999. Shortly after that antique show, Susan and I went to another California show and had a chance encounter with Las Vegas antique dealer, Neil Kohut. Neil has changed our lives. His intense background and knowledge of Steuben glass, his unerring and critical eye, coupled with his verbal inventiveness have enlivened my life. He is both my mentor and my worst critic. He is the first to compliment (rarely so it seems) and the first to criticize (frequently).

His genius for Steuben glass is unparalleled. His discerning eye is unmatched. Only Neil can spot a pin size flaw in a piece of glass from a bad photograph, or say, "Alan, it is a fake" when all the line drawings suggest it isn't. And, of course he is usually right. I have discovered the world of Carder's Steuben glass through Neil. Knowing Neil is an experience I would have hated to miss. He has given each piece of glass I've acquired special meaning. He has shared with me his talents for recognizing the artistry and beauty of perhaps the greatest glass artisan ever.

With his extraordinary knowledge of glass coupled with his gift of eloquent writing, his role as editor and collaborator was so much more than that. This is Neil's book, too.

A. N. S.

Publisher's note: The photographic details which head each section of this book are Alan and Susan Shovers' personal favorite pieces in each category. Alan's choices as his favorites are pictured to the left of the section titles; Susan's choices are to the right.

FOREWORD

CARDER'S GLASS: AN ART FORM AT ITS PINNACLE

We do not know exactly when, where, or how man first learned to make his own glass. It is generally believed, however, that the first manmade glass was in the form of a glaze on ceramic vessels, sometime in the 3000s B.C. About 1500 B.C., the first glass vessels were produced in Egypt and Mesopotamia. Since the pivotal invention of the blowpipe by an unknown person about 30 B.C., what began as a utilitarian alternative has grown, through a fascinating, ever-changing technology, to be a vehicle for a highly refined and much admired art form.

Nowhere is this art form more splendidly realized than in the hands of the gifted English designer Frederick Carder, who came to America in 1903 to work for the celebrated Steuben Company.

It is an indication of the seductive powers of Carder's alchemy that Alan Shovers and his wife Susan have brought together a collection of this substance and scope in less than six years; and we feel privileged, indeed, to be able to share these magnificent objects here.

We must recognize, too, the generosity of our Museum's longtime friends Bill and Phyllis Grimm, whose most gracious support has made this book and its attendant exhibition possible.

John W. Streetman III
Director
Evansville Museum of Arts, History & Science

PREFACE

The principal collection which constitutes this museum exhibition and forms the basis for this book is the result of two men's vision. Of course, there is Frederick Carder, the founder of The Steuben Glass Works. Then is the man who assembled this preeminent collection of Steuben glass, piece by individual piece. Without Alan Shovers' generosity and vision, there would have been no exhibition. Without his commitment to and intense admiration for Frederick Carder's Steuben glass, this collection could never have been assembled. This book and the museum exhibition which it accompanies must also be dedicated to Alan's wife, Susan. Without her exceptional eye, sense of style, and unwavering support of Alan's passion for art glass, this collection would not have achieved this level of diversity and beauty.

To amass this collection, the Shovers have traveled across America carefully selecting examples of Steuben glass at auction houses, antique shows, shops and malls. Many pieces have been hard fought for and won from online auctions, as antique collecting has rapidly evolved into a popular twenty-four hour a day, seven-day a week endeavor.

Neil Kohut
Carder Steuben collector and art glass dealer
Las Vegas, Nevada

INTRODUCTION

We begin the Twenty-first Century with our lives immersed in amazing technologies. Continually awed and inspired by our rudimentary explorations of the universe, we watch live feed pictures from Mars and Saturn and the depths of the oceans, enhanced with the finest audio and visual detail by high definition plasma and surround sound. Our homes bristle with scientific invention. Computers, electronic gadgets of every sort and kind, the promise of a wireless home; we are junkies craving for more and better buttons and perpetual upgrades always just ahead on the technology horizon.

Perhaps the hallmark of this century will be the whirling, bleeping, electronic sound of new technology rapidly grinding down to old. Yet, every generation is equally compelled by science and history to look backward, if sophomorically, to the previous pitifully primitive era from which it just emerged.

At the dawn of the Twentieth Century, mankind was still in the throes of shaking free of its earthly bonds. Engines were just beginning to move our ancestors across the land and sea with seeming effortlessness and speed. Of course there were almost no roads in fledgling America, where automobiles, steered by tillers, could travel. Electricity was just at the forefront of lighting our world and our imaginations with the fabulous flickering of technologies and inventions yet to be discovered. We marveled as indoor plumbing stretched across the nation and at the sound of the voices of neighbors and friends, who could now be connected to us by a thin wire coil, like an infinite umbilical cord extending from mouth to ear. Radio and television were still undiscovered wonders, and the world was much smaller without them. In retrospect, it was a time of industrialization and the aggressive development of new forms of communicating.

Simultaneously, America and the world were at the dawn of a different evolution, one of style, craftsmanship and artistic rebirth. Old world craftsmen were combining their ideas of beauty and style with modern production techniques that brought art into the home of the average citizen. Furniture, glass and pottery could be produced by hand or with applied artistic flourishes in vast factories, which, for the first time, would make art for the masses, and would come to dominate the first half of the century with great benchmarks of art and design.

That merger of art and industry we call art glass is the topic of this book, which explores the influences and products of talented and inspiring men like Emile Gallé, Louis Comfort Tiffany, René Lalique and Frederick Carder. These men and a host of their contemporaries would build factories attracting workmen bearing an incredible mastery of glassmaking skills and the ability to train their replacements to perpetuate and innovate throughout subsequent decades.

This story focuses on Frederick Carder, who stands as a giant among the art geniuses of his time, for his stunning achievements crossing eight decades of the century's artistic tapestry. Constrained by the styles of Victorian England, Carder traveled to America in 1903 to form Steuben Glass. At forty, he was a classically trained artist with nearly thirty years of experience working with and designing glass. Those talents would flourish in the cauldron of creativity that was early Twentieth Century America. This book will take you on an awesome journey in pictures, through the great design eras that highlighted his long and artistically prolific life. As the popularity of his timeless designs, brilliant colors and creative techniques make new friends in the Twenty-first Century, his unique legacy will continue to grow as one of the great glass artists of all time.

Well thought out collections like this one, assembled by Susan and Alan Shovers, seek to preserve that legacy for new generations to study and enjoy. Their generosity in sharing this formidable collection with us, through the auspices of the Evansville Museum of Arts, History & Science, is greatly appreciated. This accompanying book will serve to memorialize the greatness of Frederick Carder and the glass produced under his aegis at Steuben. The Shovers fervently hope their collection inspires you and fires you with their passion to learn more about Steuben, and perhaps even start your own collection.

Neil Kohut
Carder Steuben collector and art glass dealer
Las Vegas, Nevada

AN APPRECIATION

Few knew it at the time, but early March, 1903, was destined to become an important time in the history of American decorative arts for it was then that an English glassmaker named Frederick Carder stepped off a ship at New York City. Less than two weeks later, it was publicly announced that he and Thomas G. Hawkes of American cut glass fame were opening a new glass factory in the little upstate New York community of Corning. This was the beginning of an adventure in American art glass without parallel. This was the beginning of Steuben Glass.

Frederick Carder came to America well-equipped to run a glass works and produce beautiful art glass. He had worked at Stevens & Williams, one of England's premier glass companies, as a glass designer and chemist since 1880. In 1903, when Carder came to America, he was already recognized by the English glassmaking world as a successful leader, teacher, and artist. Frederick Carder brought to America not only skills and experience in glassmaking and design, but also a philosophy and personal understanding of art that grew from the experiences of his English glassmaking years. Perhaps the strongest beliefs he brought to America had their genesis in the English Arts and Crafts movement, a movement which led Carder to believe in craftsmanship almost to the point of worshipping it. This belief, plus his life-long commitment to glass, to quality and to the beauty of good design, defined what Steuben is all about and has been since 1903. Carder wrote about his strong feelings regarding craftsmanship and quality often. In 1923, for instance, he wrote about what was happening in the manufacture of American glass.

> Other factories have since turned their attention to the making of colored glass, one or two making a good product, while others are making it cheap and hasty—this latter tendency on the part of some American glass manufacturers is deplorable, and, as in the case of cut glass some years ago, can mean only one thing, *ruin to the industry.*

> As [John] Ruskin said, "A disposition for cheapness and not for excellence of workmanship is the most frequent and certain cause of decay and destruction of arts and manufacturers."

> Let us hope that the American manufacturers will look to it that this beautiful art craft is fostered and encouraged. (Frederick Carder, "Artistic Glassware," Journal of the American Ceramic Society, January, 1923, 231.)

Frederick Carder has left us much. He has enriched all of our lives. He has given us Steuben, a company that continues to this very day to produce beautiful art glass emphasizing craftsmanship, quality, and design. During his tenure at Steuben from 1903 to 1932, Carder, as a glass chemist, created over 140 colors and types of Steuben glass including Aurene, Cluthra, Cintra, Florentia, Ivrene, and Moresque to mention just a few. As a designer during this same period, he designed some 8,000 shapes to be made as Steuben objects.

Carder's creativity, knowledge, talent, skill, and productivity over his 80-year career in art glass have left museums, collectors, artists, glassmakers, students, historians and all Americans a rich legacy. His eclecticism in design resulted in his designs reflecting influences from all parts of the world and all time periods and styles. Amazingly, these designs remain relatively timeless and reflect a uniqueness that is Carder's. His range of techniques of glassmaking also spans all of glass history. Frederick Carder believed that glass was a wondrous thing given almost a life of its own by its ability to reflect and refract and transmit light. He also believed that it was color that could then escalate the innate beauty of glass to greater and greater heights.

Frederick Carder's creations offer much. Perhaps most importantly, however, his life and his creations constantly remind us of the importance of beauty, craftsmanship, and quality. How much more can we ask.

Thomas P. Dimitroff
Honorary Curator, the Rockwell Museum, Frederick Carder Collection
Corning, New York

TABLE OF CONTENTS

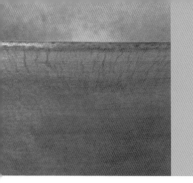

My First Favorite Piece of Art Glass

I am always asked the question, "How long did it take you to assemble such a vast and varied collection?" Susan is always asked, "Who dusts all of this?" The answers are easy. My grand passion for collecting Carder Steuben glass began about six years ago, aided by luck, timing and internet relationships with dealers and other collectors willing to part with a piece or two of their prized collections. And I dust it all. Susan attempts to turn our glass museum into a home for the people who live in it. We don't always agree on which pieces should occupy "most favored status" in our household, but we both concede that we are running out of space to display these wonderful art glass treasures.

For many years, Susan and I collected mass produced black amethyst glass. This glass was manufactured by several American glass companies and was relatively easy to find. We loved these varied shapes and sizes and integrated these pieces into our decor using black as the accent color. We amassed a good-sized collection of about 800 pieces snatched from antique stores, flea markets and house sales. We shared the joy of the hunt and the fun of finding a really terrific new piece. We used the vases for flowers and the compotes for candy throughout our home. The decorating effect in our home was stunning.

The Carder Steuben transformation really began during a vacation trip to San Diego. We decided to go to the Del Mar Antique Show in hopes of finding some more black glass. Instead, I was captivated by an elegant gold iridescent bowl, perched simply and gracefully on a table in one of the booths. I couldn't stop looking at it. This was no ordinary piece of glass. There was some kind of a sorcerer's spell. I was mesmerized. The piece was extraordinary and clearly an astounding glass art achievement, beyond anything I had previously witnessed.

The dealer identified it as Steuben, called Gold Aurene. He had me hold it so I could touch and feel the quality of the glass. It was made in the twenties and designed by Frederick Carder for Steuben Glass Works. Although I longed to have it, the incredible asking price of $2,000 far exceeded any of my previous purchases. I walked away–hands empty, but mind filled with the imprint of this glorious piece of glass. I thought about this Gold Aurene bowl for months. I talked about it. I dreamt about it. I began researching Carder Steuben, buying books and learning as much as I could. The piece became my quest. Finally Susan said, "If you love it, you should buy it" (she always says that). So we flew out for the next Del Mar Antique Show and raced directly to the same dealer's booth.

There it sat, my magnificent Gold Aurene bowl, simple, classic and elegant. I bought it. It is still my most favorite piece of art glass. Well, okay, it was only the beginning of collecting my favorite art glass pieces.

The pieces, especially the rare ones, are difficult to find. As rewarding as that is, the real fun is the "hunt".

Alan Shovers
Evansville, Indiana

GOLD AURENE CENTERPIECE BOWL
5 1/2 Inches High, 13 7/8 Inches Wide
Shape #2851, p. 142 Gardner, *Fn*

Fn. All shape numbers referred to are factory numbers. They can be found in the form of line drawings in The Glass of Frederick Carder, by Paul V. Gardner, from pages 137 to 342.

FREDERICK C. CARDER 1863-1963
"Life is Short, Art is Long"

Several momentous coincidences occurred at Stevens & Williams Glass Works, as the Twentieth Century dawned in England. Frederick Carder had spent more than twenty years at Stevens & Williams as a chief designer and draftsman under John Northwood. The relationship between the two men had become strained and when Mr. Northwood died in 1902, his son was named to succeed him as art director and works manager. Mr. Carder now faced the likelihood that at thirty-nine years of age, having been passed over for the promotion he wanted, he was now locked in a job with no possibility for advancement.

So, the next year, when the opportunity presented itself for him to travel to America to report on how the glass trade was conducted here, he jumped at the opportunity. Within a day of arriving in Corning, New York he had struck a deal with Thomas Hawkes to form a new company that would produce glass blanks for Mr. Hawkes' cutting shop. Mr. Hawkes had been buying blanks from Stevens & Williams as well as other glass houses since 1880. This new enterprise was to be named Steuben Glass Works, after its namesake, Steuben County, New York.

Freed from the constraints of designing glass for someone else, Mr. Carder embarked on his most creative and prodigious period. Over the next thirty years, he would design more than seven thousand shapes; create a hundred plus colors and a similar number of techniques. There would also be about one hundred fifty patterns for cut, engraved and etched glass. This output was astounding and unprecedented in the industry.

Over the years he proved astute and adaptable in combining his training as a classical artist with the popular trends of the day. He would master them, one and all, and was at the forefront of glass design for all of his thirty years as Steuben's head. In no small part, as a result of Mr. Carder's efforts, this became the golden age for American art glass.

When forced from his position at Steuben in 1933, the then sixty-nine-year-old began his "studio" period. Corning Glass Works, Steuben's then owner, provided him with a studio, an assistant and the resources to do as he pleased. For roughly twenty-five years, Mr. Carder would develop a process for casting glass in the same manner that metals were cast into statuary. The "Lost Wax" process, as it was known, had never been fully explored in glass, although the French artist, René Lalique had some limited success with it.

The successful development of this Lost Wax technique resulted in magnificent limited production and one-of-a-kind statues in clear crystal that were a showcase for Mr. Carder's sculpture. In his nineties, this work culminated with the creation of Diatreta, a copy of ancient Roman caged glass in which a design was back carved away from the main body of the glass, creating a cage-like outer design suspended by studs connecting to the vase or bowl. In Roman times, this amazing effect was created with laborious hand carving from a single piece of glass. Mr. Carder cast these intricate designs in one casting, using colored glass cullet, a feat which has never been duplicated. As he perfected the technique, the design of the cage became more intricate, even employing tens of miniature cherubic figures.

This book presents several hundred photographs which serve to showcase a small fraction of the vast creativity and innovation that Mr. Carder brought to this art form. His abilities were so vast that this presentation is but a limited view into the genius of Frederick Carder and his wonderful Steuben glass.

"WINTER IS NOT FAR BEHIND"
25 Inches High by 21 Inches Wide

Oil on gesso board dated 1960, and signed on the back "Fred'k Carder". Age 96 or 97.

After age 90 and into his late 90s, Mr. Carder was painting in oil and watercolor.

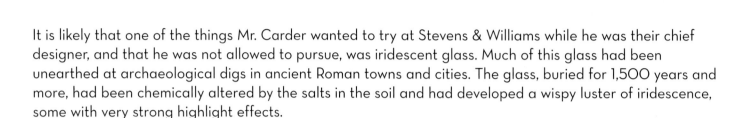

Gold Aurene

It is likely that one of the things Mr. Carder wanted to try at Stevens & Williams while he was their chief designer, and that he was not allowed to pursue, was iridescent glass. Much of this glass had been unearthed at archaeological digs in ancient Roman towns and cities. The glass, buried for 1,500 years and more, had been chemically altered by the salts in the soil and had developed a wispy luster of iridescence, some with very strong highlight effects.

Tiffany and Loetz had already developed this technique and were using it to win awards and accolades worldwide. A gold iridescent glass was one of the first glasses that Mr. Carder attempted as soon as the furnaces were up and running at Steuben. The first trial piece was executed in 1904 at his new Steuben factory.

While it was a milestone for him, it was actually just a first step in an evolutionary process during which his Aurene would strengthen in color, brilliance and sheen. The early Aurene, as seen on pages 6 through 9, had soft colors that were true to the look of the unearthed Roman glass. Over the years it became so much more, as seen in the centerpiece bowl pictured at page 13. While collectors today adore the brilliant highlights of blue, pink and red strongly emphasized against a glowing gold iridescence, they revere those early, subtly colored pieces even more. The importance of Steuben's gold iridescent glass is such that even its proprietary name Aurene has found its way into our lexicon to describe iridescent glass from every maker.

EARLY PERIOD THREE STEM VASE
8 3/4 Inches High
Shape #186

In 1904 Art Nouveau was the trend in art glass. Organic foliate forms, sinuous lines, and non-geometric, "whiplash" curves were the style. Mr. Carder, having recently founded his Steuben Glass Works, was hard at work experimenting and creating Gold Aurene and beginning his prolific designing. From this arises one of h early Aurene pieces. We know this from the low shape number of 186 and the early soft Aurene look. This va fits perfectly into the movement of the time, with its grace, perfect symmetry and balance. This is mastery of the movement, while still maintaining the integrity of Mr. Carder's classic training. Imagine the difficulty of th master glass blowers trying to work with hot glass and creating perfectly even and proportional spidery leg Perhaps this unique design for Mr. Carder, which is rarely seen and not followed by him in later designs, suggests the struggles of trial and error that took place on the glass blowing factory floor.

EARLY PERIOD PINCHED VASE WITH FOUR PRUNTS c. 1905
4 1/2 Inches High
Shape #150

PINCHED VASE c. 1905
7 Inches High
Shape #136

BOUDOIR LAMP WITH MATCHING GLASS BASE AND SHADE

13 Inches High

Shape #915

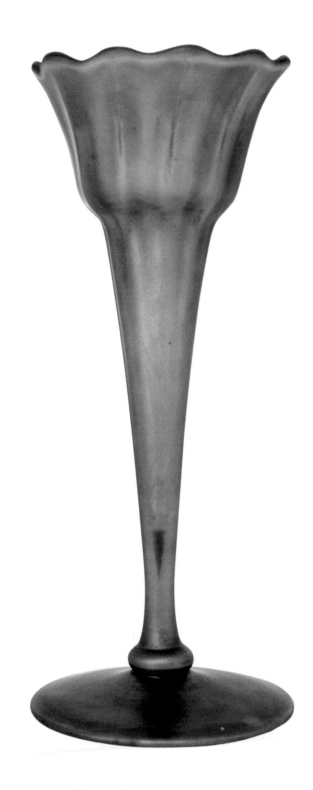

EARLY PERIOD GOLD AURENE VASE
5 Inches High
Shape #561

An Aurene's iridescent surface comes from spraying the glass with stannous chloride or lead chloride and reheating it under controlled atmospheric conditions.

FLORIFORM VASE
4 3/4 Inches High
Shape #2652

OPEN SALT DISH WITH SWIRLED RIBBING AND PULLED DECORATION
1 1/2 Inches High, 2 Inches Diameter
Shape #706

PINCHED BOWL WITH EIGHT FLOWER HOLDERS
3 1/2 Inches High, 8 Inches Diameter
Shape #2775

BASKET WITH SWIRLED PRUNTS &
BASKET WITH BERRY PRUNTS
9 Inches High, Shape #453
4 1/2 Inches High, Shape #455

It has been suggested that the miniature basket could be a salt that was part of a Haviland china tableware set. However, the shape number suggests it was designed prior to the Haviland period, although it still could have been incorporated into a Haviland purchase.

CENTERPIECE BOWL WITH SCULPTURED FOOT
6 Inches High
Shape #6058

STOCKING DARNER
6 1/2 Inches Long
Whimsey

GOLD AURENE ARCHITECTURAL TILE c. 1924
3 1/2 Inches Point to Point
Shape #A2121

This historical tile was salvaged from the main entryway of Corning Glass Works Building #21 when it was razed in 1993.

DIAMOND QUILTED CREAMER AND OPEN SUGAR
Creamer 4 Inches High
Sugar 2 1/4 Inches High
Both Shape #252

Optic molds were commonly used at Steuben to give the glass a pattern. The more commonly found ones were diamond quilts, swirls and vertical panels. After blowing a gather of glass into the appropriate mold, glass was then hand blown and shaped into the finished product.

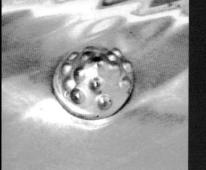

Of all the colors and techniques manufactured at Steuben, none seems to have a more universal appeal than Blue Aurene. Once you have seen it you are likely to be forever captivated and charmed by it. As with Gold Aurene, the Blue evolved from a pale color, almost platinum, to the color and shimmering iridescence of butterfly wings or peacock feathers. Unlike similar wares from other makers, Mr. Carder's version has a slightly greenish cast which adds a unique complexity to the iridescence and sets it apart. Highlights can range from green to the most incredibly rich purples that are sure to dazzle the viewer.

BLUE AURENE SCALLOPED RIM AND TWIST STEM COMPOTE
8 Inches High
Shape #367

The twist stem is one of the most admired and collected of Mr. Carder's designs. It appears in vases, candlesticks, compotes and stemware of all kinds. This Early period Blue Aurene with its soft iridescence has an onion skin effect. These minute cracks in the iridescent coating occur when the object is manipulated and shaped after a final tin and iron chloride spray are applied.

MELON RIBBED FOOTED BATH SALT
4 1/4 Inches High
Shape #2701

VASE WITH BERRY PRUNTS AND OPTIC SWIRL PATTERN
4 1/4 Inches Wide, 3 Inches High
Shape #781

VASE WITH APPLIED SCROLLED HANDLES
12 Inches High
Shape #6630

FOOTED VASE WITH THREE APPLIED SCROLLED HANDLES
6 1/2 Inches High
Shape #6627

COVERED FOOTED VASES
6 1/4 Inches High (left)
Shape #2822
5 1/2 Inches High (right)
Shape #2824

DEEPLY RIBBED LAMP FROM KAPLAN, INC.
28 1/2 Inches High
Shape #6218

The body and foot are two separate pieces of glass assembled into the metal lamp fittings. Note: The top portion of the body incorporates a traditional Blue Aurene finish and a Platinum finish on one piece of glass.

PERFUME
7 Inches High (left)
Shape #3294

DECANTER
9 1/2 Inches High (right)
Shape #2953

BOWL WITH RIBBING
6 3/4 Inches Wide, 3 Inches High
Shape #564

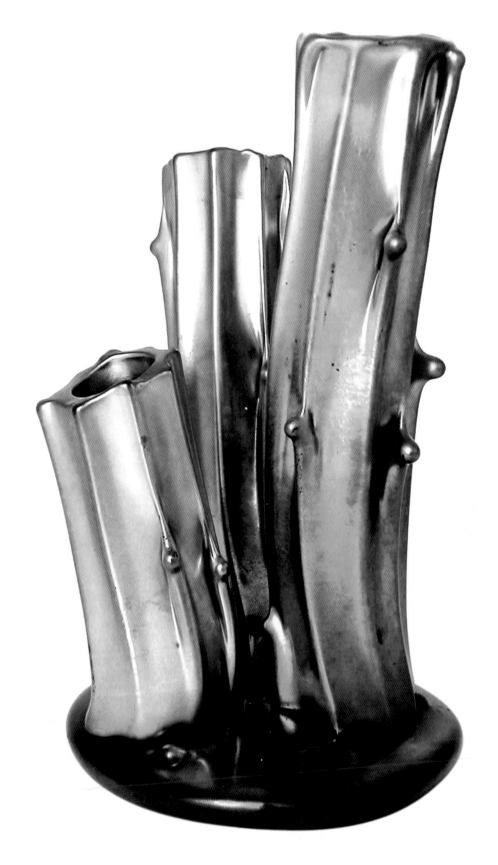

THREE PRONG RUSTIC OR STUMP TYPE BUD VASE
6 Inches High
Shape #2744

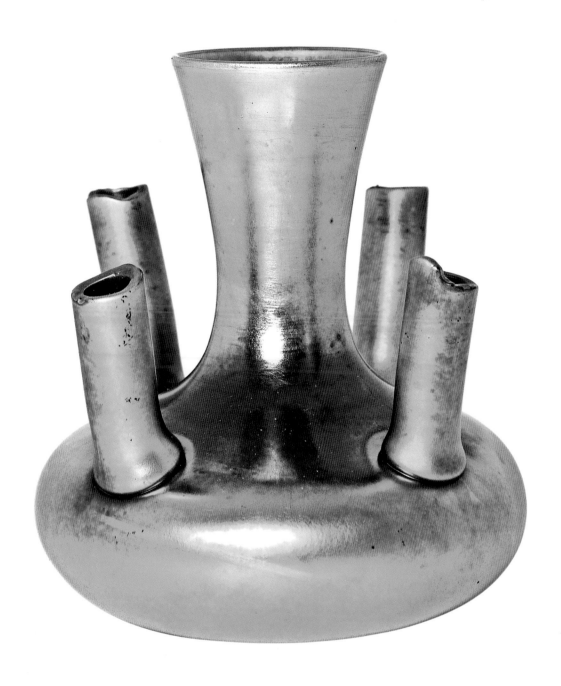

BUD VASE

4 Inches High

Shape #2837

Decorated Aurenes

The first ten years at Steuben saw the creation of many different colors of glass with iridized finishes. We have already seen the Blue and Gold Aurenes in previous sections. Other known iridized colors are green, mirror black, red, brown, yellow and amethyst. Calcite, turquoise, alabaster and green jade were also iridized, but today we do not recognize these as Aurenes nor are Verre de Soie or Ivrene considered Aurenes. While these fine distinctions may be confusing to the casual observer, they have stood the test of time.

A piece of art glass may be decorated in many ways. This section will discuss and illustrate some of the ways in which iridized glassware was decorated at Steuben. Decorations were done at the fire by applying colored glass threads and circles to the nearly completed object. These appliqués were manipulated with a metal hook and pulled into the desired decoration. By hooking the threads in opposite directions, they could be formed into loops, or varying types of feathers. By pulling the hook once through a circle of glass, a heart or leaf shape could be fashioned. Millefiori glass florets and other flower shapes were also applied to some of these decorated Aurenes.

In execution it was actually a lot simpler than it would appear to be. Once the appliqués were hooked into their final design, the decoration was marvered or pressed into the body of the piece until it was smooth. A later variant on this technique only marvered the design partially into the glass leaving a striking raised effect.

Decorated Aurenes, as well as decorated iridized calcite and alabaster, are perhaps the most highly prized category of Steuben glass commonly available to today's collectors. While ranging from very scarce to extremely rare, they represent some of the most exciting art glass ever produced at Steuben. Fortunately, decorated Aurenes were produced in great numbers as lamp shades. In addition to being far more readily available to the collector, these shades are considerably lower in price and can carry decorations never seen on non-shade forms.

FAN VASE
8 3/4 Inches High
Shape #6297

After a ten year period during which decorated Aurenes had not been produced, Mr. Carder reintroduced them. These late period decorated Aurenes were only available in gold or blue. Forms were clean and modern, reflecting the tastes of the roaring twenties, and the decoration was a very straightforward heart and vine pattern that was often left slightly raised from the glass body. The examples, above and on the next two pages, represent the late period decorated Aurenes. Interestingly, Mr. Carder didn't feel his Aurenes needed this further embellishment. *Fn*

Fn. Frederick Carder: Portrait of a Glassmaker by Paul V. Gardner, p.23.

AURENE VASES WITH LEAF-AND-VINE DECORATION

6 3/8 Inches High
Shape #6299
(left)

8 7/8 Inches High
Shape #6297
(right)

1920s decorated Aurene vases will be found with the leaf-and-vine ornamentation or Guilloche (chain) decoration.

TWO EXAMPLES OF GREEN GUILLOCHE (CHAIN) DECORATION ON AURENE

7 1/2 inches High
Shape #6177

This is a late period decoration used only briefly.

**FOOTED FLORIFORM VASE WITH
LEAF-AND-VINE DECORATION AND
APPLIED MILLEFIORI FLORETS**
8 Inches High
Shape #542, Style "D"

**LONG STEMMED FLORIFORM
VASE WITH PULLED
FEATHER DECORATION**
10 1/2 Inches High
Shape #215, Style "B"

GOLD AURENE VASE AND "PLATINUM" AURENE VASE WITH TRAILED LEAF-AND-VINE AND MILLEFIORI FLORETS DECORATION

5 Inches High
Shape #573, Style "J"

These charming vases exemplify a style of decoration used at Steuben and Tiffany around 1915. The addition of Millefiori florets to the ornamentation suggests flowering vines. While both vases bear the same factory shape number and Gold Aurene coloration, when these handmade pieces are shown side by side, they show considerable variation. The vase on the left exhibits the classic coloration of early Gold Aurene while the one on the right has a distinct silvery blue tone and blue highlights. Many enthusiasts believe this coloration shift was done deliberately to create a platinum colored Aurene. Others believe that both vases are Gold Aurene and that the platinum one was just an aberration caused during production. Paul V. Gardner says that the name Platinum Aurene was not found in the factory records. Rather he says that Gold Aurene sometimes developed a silvery tone and when found they seem to be erroneously called Platinum Aurene. *Fn*

Fn. Frederick Carder: Portrait of a Glassmaker by Paul V. Gardner, p.64.

BLUE AURENE VASE WITH PEACOCK FEATHER DECORATION
4 1/2 Inches High
Shape #734

This vase is an example of an early piece of Blue Aurene c. 1905. The early pieces have a soft platinum-like sheen and subdued coloration. Later pieces were richer in color and more electric in their iridescence. Examples of early decorated Blue Aurene are extremely rare.

IRIDIZED TURQUOISE VASE WITH GOLD AURENE
PULLED AND HOOKED FEATHER DECORATION
5 3/4 Inches High
Shape #655

BROWN AURENE VASE WITH INTARSIA COLLAR
13 1/4 Inches High
Shape #2737

RED AURENE VASE WITH FLOWER DECORATION

9 Inches High

Shape #270

COVERED LUMINOR IN CALCITE
WITH PULLED FEATHERS OF GOLD, RUBY AND BLUE
13 Inches High
Shape #2805

This decoration of semi overlapping pulled feathers is scarce and seems to be limited to a few shapes of these calcite covered luminors and vases. Where the colored threads overlap, the colors seems to join together forming purples. There is a high degree of difficulty in the precision of overlayed feathering, but the result of all this delicate and intricate work is mesmerizing.

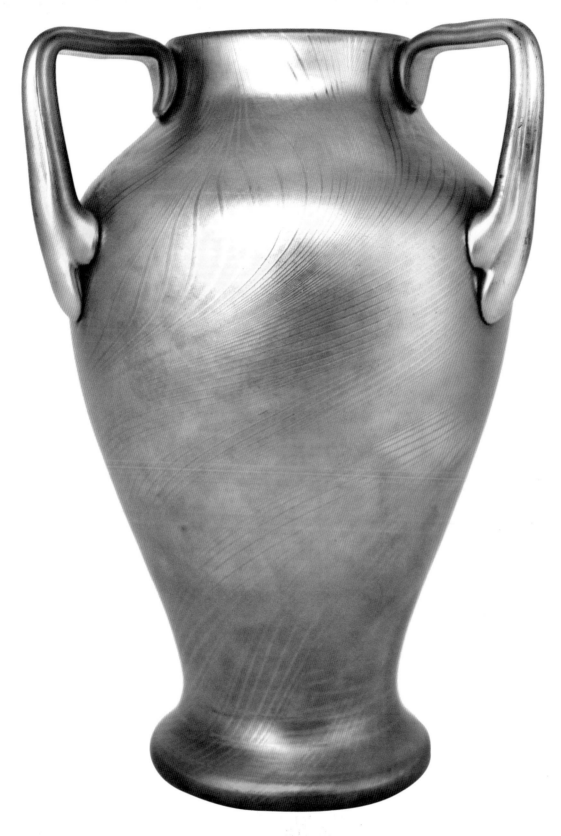

**GOLD AURENE VASE WITH GREEN PULLED TRAILINGS DECORATION
AND THREE APPLIED HANDLES**

8 1/4 Inches High

Shape #758

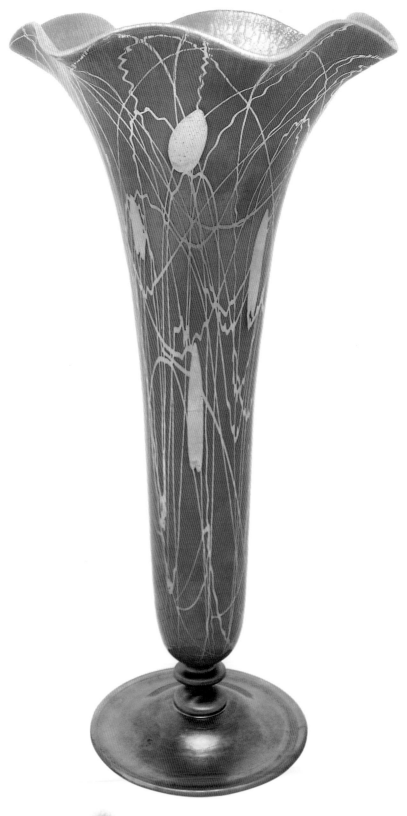

GOLD RUBY FOOTED FLORIFORM VASE DECORATED WITH GOLD AURENE LEAF AND RANDOM VINE DECORATION

12 1/4 Inches High
Shape #547, Style "E"

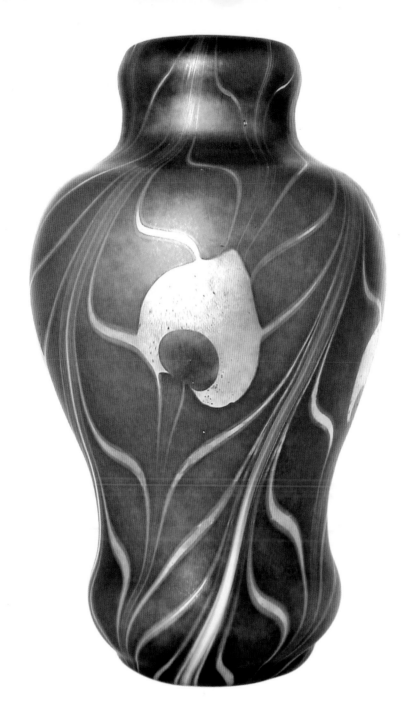

GREEN AURENE VASE WITH PEACOCK FEATHER DECORATION
8 Inches High
Shape #508, Style "O"

The above Green Aurene vase and those on the next several pages are comprised of three glass layers. The white calcite core glass gives the green outer casing a canvas from which it really can show off its incredible color. The inside casing of topaz, when iridized, adds a richness that we associate with Gold Aurene. The decoration is applied near the end of manufacture and is marvered or pressed into the glass until the surface is as smooth as a single piece of glass. The process of casing glass is difficult and requires a master glassmaker to control the heat and the layers of glass to prevent them from separating or forming bubbles. The results are well worth the effort.

DECORATED GREEN VASE WITH GOLD AURENE HEART AND TRAILING VINES
4 1/2 Inches High
Shape #543, Style "D"

**DECORATED GREEN ON CALCITE
WITH GOLD AURENE PULLED FEATHER DECORATION**
5 1/2 Inches High
Shape #546, Style "G"

DECORATED GREEN ON CALCITE WITH GOLD AURENE PULLED FEATHER AND DRAG LOOP DECORATION

9 1/2 Inches High

Shape #296

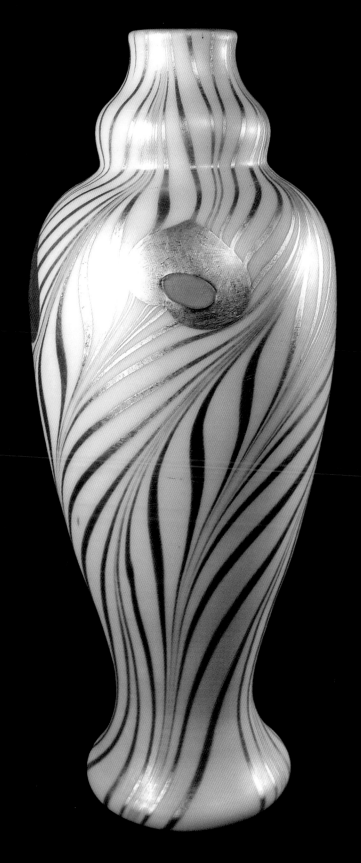

CALCITE VASE WITH PEACOCK FEATHER DECORATION
10 Inches High
Shape #267

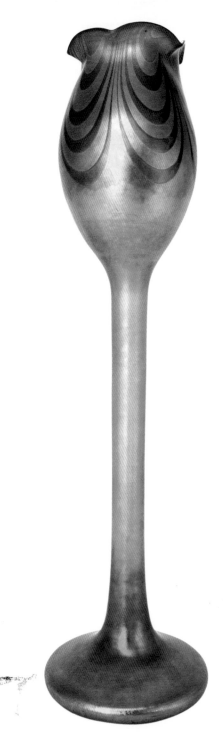

GOLD AURENE VASE WITH DRAG LOOP DECORATION
15 inches High
Shape #195B

When Mr. Carder began his work at Steuben in the early 1900s he incorporated the Art Nouveau movement with floral and foliate motifs. He prided himself on designing dozens of flower forms from memory. Undoubtedly this is the result of his love of nature and his art school training. This iridescent Floriform shaped vase with undulating rim has a drape pattern of green on platinum hued Gold Aurene. The vase combines elements of nature in a soft Gold Aurene typical of its early coloration. The stateliness of this lovely tulip shape is enhanced by this vase's imposing height of 15 inches.

**GOLD AURENE VASE WITH GREEN PULLED TRAILINGS
AND PEACOCK DECORATION**

10 3/4 Inches High

Shape #255

Iridescence

A wide range of iridescent glassware was produced at Steuben in addition to the ever popular Aurenes. Some of the iridescent techniques have grown in popularity while others have suffered the misfortune to fall out of favor. This section opens with Oriental Poppy and Oriental Jade. These two color variants of the same technique are enjoying a tremendous popularity and are becoming prohibitively priced. This technique has sixteen alternating vertical stripes of opalescent and either pink (Oriental Poppy), green (Oriental Jade), or a third very hard to find color, amethyst (Oriental Orchid).

An unusual Oriental Poppy variant is shown on the next page. The applied green band and rim as well as the absence of any iridescence make this piece quite rare. This technique was extended to table service where Mr. Carder threw a few more twists into the mix. Stemware, plates and sherbets were most commonly not iridized and the stripes would frequently spiral around the piece as opposed to the vertical stripes seen here.

This section will also cover Verre de Soie, Ivrene and Iridized Green Jade. Verre de Soie has been widely reported to be Mr. Carder's favorite. By iridizing clear crystal, a rainbow of colors may be seen dancing across the surface of the glass. The colors are commonly pretty subtle and are reminiscent of the fleeting sheen found on a soap bubble.

Ivrene seems to have fallen from the public's favor, which is a shame because it was a late term introduction that lent itself beautifully to the Art Deco forms that Mr. Carder produced so successfully. Ivrene's iridescence shifts mostly toward pastel pinks and blues. Finally, Iridized Green Jade is the least obtainable glass in this iridescent group. It may require years of searching to find a single example. Generally the iridescence in Iridized Green Jade is very soft, but the addition of Gold Aurene reeding at the top of these pieces gives them a unique appeal.

ORIENTAL POPPY VASE VARIANT, NOT IRIDIZED, WITH APPLIED GREEN RIM
5 Inches High
Shape #6638

ORIENTAL POPPY VASES

5 Inches High (front)
Shape #6500

6 Inches High (back)
Shape #6501

ORIENTAL JADE VASE

5 Inches High
Shape #6500

ORIENTAL POPPY CONSOLE SET, NOT IRIDIZED
Compote 6 1/2 Inches High, Candlesticks 6 Inches High
Shape #6614

VERRE DE SOIE PITCHER WITH IRIDIZED BLACK REEDING
9 1/4 Inches High
Shape #7199

VERRE DE SOIE DIAMOND QUILTED VASE WITH FRENCH BLUE REEDING
8 Inches High
Shape #6813

VERRE DE SOIE VASE WITH THREE APPLIED HANDLES
6 Inches High
Shape #766

VERRE DE SOIE COVERED COMPOTE WITH RED CINTRA PEAR FINIAL
AND IRIDIZED CELESTE BLUE STEM

6 3/4 Inches High
Shape #3343

AQUAMARINE TUMBLE UP ENGRAVED ON BOTH PIECES
6 1/4 Inches Tall
Shape #3064

Aquamarine is one of three variants of Steuben's Verre de Soie. Aquamarine is Verre de Soie on a pale, bottle green glass. Cyprian has the addition of applied turquoise rims. A very few examples of Verre de Soie in other colors have surfaced over the years. These may have been trial pieces that never entered production. By iridizing only very lightly colored glass ,Mr. Carder was able to maintain the overall appearance of Verre de Soie.

Tumble ups were a Victorian fancy that Mr. Carder brought with him from Stevens & Williams. They were designed to be kept on the nightstand. The tumbler was cleverly inverted and stored inside the neck of the pitcher, hence the name tumble up. This was not only convenient, but kept the water free from dust and insects.

IRIDIZED GREEN JADE VASE WITH GOLD AURENE REEDING

7 1/2 Inches High

Shape #6034

IRIDIZED GREEN JADE VASE WITH GOLD AURENE REEDING
11 Inches High
Shape #6814

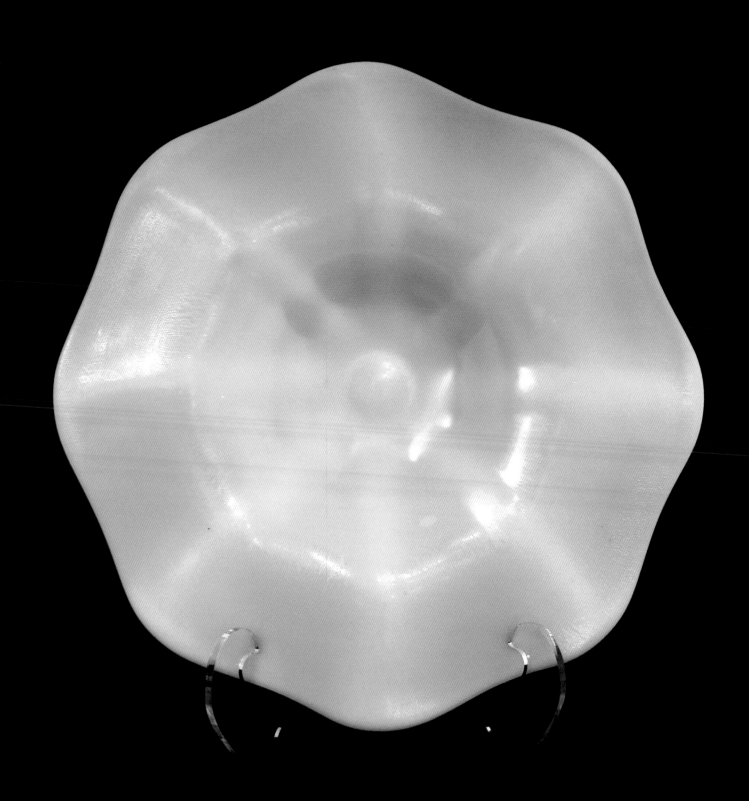

IVRENE CHARGER SIZED PLATE
15 1/3 Inches Wide
Shape #7561

Cintra

In 1915 Mr. Carder developed Cintra glass. Cintra is created by picking up crushed and powdered colored glass on a gather of clear crystal which encases the particles. Frequently a fine matrix of bubbles was enclosed in the clear crystal layer.

ORANGE CINTRA COMPOTE WITH TURQUOISE ACCENTS ON RIM AND FOOT
7 1/2 Inches High
Shape #3179

FACETED CRYSTAL PAPERWEIGHT STYLE COLOGNE BOTTLE WITH PINK TO BLUE SHADED CINTRA INTERNAL DECORATION AND CONTROLLED BUBBLES

11 Inches High

Shape #6687

Glass paperweights gained popularity in the mid-Nineteenth Century and remain just as popular today. They usually consisted of colorful decorations, perhaps with bubbles, encased in a thick layer of fine crystal, which created the illusion that the decoration was floating in space. Decorations could consist of flowers, millefiori canes, writing, hearts, crosses, ribbons, leaves or any combination of those elements. Mr. Carder brought the paperweight to Steuben in the form of a heavy cologne bottle, as he extended the paperweight concept to a new creative high. In this Paperweight Cologne Bottle Mr. Carder artfully blended the exquisitely beautiful bubbly pinks, blues and purples of the internal Cintra decoration with a sparkling clear, faceted crystal that has bubbles dancing through it in a controlled pattern. Few of these cologne bottles were produced and they varied in color, decoration and facet style.

HEAVY CUT CRYSTAL PAPERWEIGHT STYLE COLOGNE BOTTLE
INTERNAL CINTRA DECORATION OF TWO TONED GREEN LEAVES
AND CIRCLES OVER A MATRIX OF FINE BUBBLES
8 3/4 Inches High
Shape #6708

This sculptured paperweight cologne combines bold deep cut work to the clear crystal exterior. The internal leaves resemble the technique Mr. Carder used in his Florentia decoration, coupled with a Venetian style chain decoration in an Art Deco piece. The green decoration appears to float on the surface of the internal random bubbled glass.

OPALESCENT GLASS VASE ACID CUT TO GREEN CINTRA
IN ASTRID PATTERN
15 1/4 Inches High
Shape #8415

The soft coloration and finish of this particularly tall vase combine several highly desirable glass forms and techniques. The base layer is green Cintra glass. The Cintra is cased with opalescent glass. Then the opalescent is acid cut to form the Astrid pattern. Finally, acid is applied to the pattern to bring it to a satin finish.

FRENCH BLUE CINTRA PERFUME AND PUFF BOX

Puff Box 3 Inches High
Puff Box Shape #2910

Perfume 7 Inches High
Perfume Shape #3294

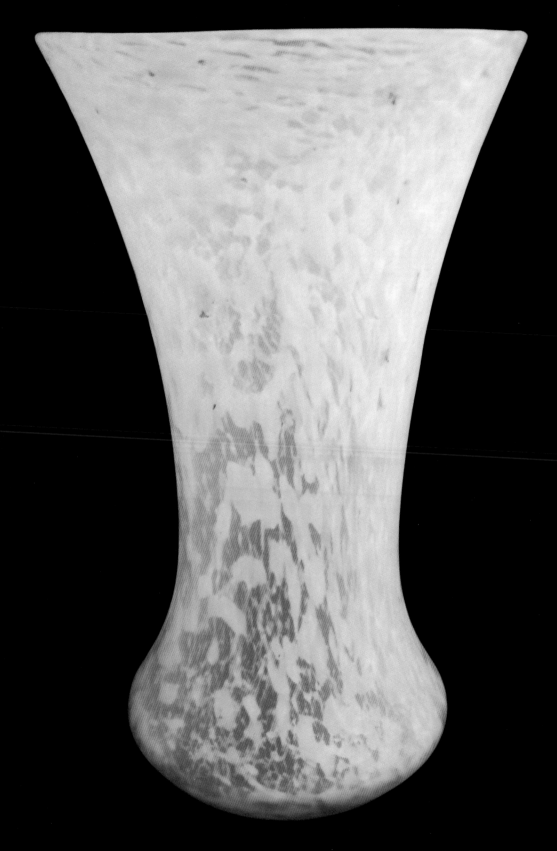

GREEN CINTRA VASE WITHOUT BUBBLES

12 Inches High

Shape #6812

Cluthra

Cluthra is an amazing concoction. A first time observer may end up being transfixed by all the activity within the glass. Cased between two thick layers of clear crystal lies a mottled layer of colored glass, achieved by rolling a parison of clear crystal onto a marver of powdered and crushed glass. This was either alabaster or alabaster in combination with either Pomona Green, Celeste Blue, Cardinal Red, Amethyst or Black. An agent was introduced into this color layer that caused large, random bubbles to form. It has been suspected that this agent might have been tapioca.

An outer casing of clear crystal was applied and the bubbles would grow within the hot glass. As they expanded, the bubbles pushed the colored glass aside causing rivulets and eddies of white and other colors to form around the bubbles, many of which took on the appearance of eyes. Some Cluthra, like the example pictured below, shaded from one of the named colors to alabaster. In appearance, this is a very dramatic and desirable effect.

GROUPING OF ROSE CLUTHRA ITEMS SHADED TO WHITE

Cologne, 5 1/2 Inches High
Shape #6881

Finger Bowl & Underplate, 2 1/2 Inches High
Shape # 6909

Vase, 10 1/4 Inches High
Shape #6926

Three Prong Vase on Clear Crystal Foot (illustrated on previous page), **10 Inches High**
Shape #6873

RED CLUTHRA VASE
13 Inches High
Shape #8494

Shape numbers in the 8000 series were usually special order pieces. This vase is cased with an outer layer of transparent green over rose, creating this unique Cluthra red color. The color combination may be seen at the lip of the vase. Because Cluthra is not usually cased in a transparent color, it has been speculated that this vase was originally intended to be acid cut.

GREEN CLUTHRA VASE WITH OPALESCENT "M" SHAPED HANDLES
10 Inches High
Shape #8508

Acid Etched

In the late Nineteenth Century the English were making incredible carved glass works of art fashioned after the ancient Portland vase. These cameo glass pieces were being crafted while a young Frederick Carder was applying his ideas to the production at Stevens & Williams. He worked under the tutelage of the highly respected John Northwood.

He and Mr. Northwood designed and crafted some of the finest cameo glass ever made; and a team of expert glassmakers rarely assembled up to that time executed other examples, some of which took weeks to carve.

This was the cauldron that forged Mr. Carder's love of glass and its intriguing play of light and color. Cameo glass was so cost prohibitive that many glass houses started using acid cutting, at first combined with wheel polishing and detailing, and later just acid cutting. Most of the glass produced was repetitive and gradually faded from favor; that is, with the exception of the work that Frederick Carder was producing at Steuben.

Most of the colors and techniques he created for Steuben ended up in the treasured acid cut pieces. The process was timeless, but the style was all Frederick Carder. Nowhere is his skill and talent better revealed than in the vast array of acid cut pieces.

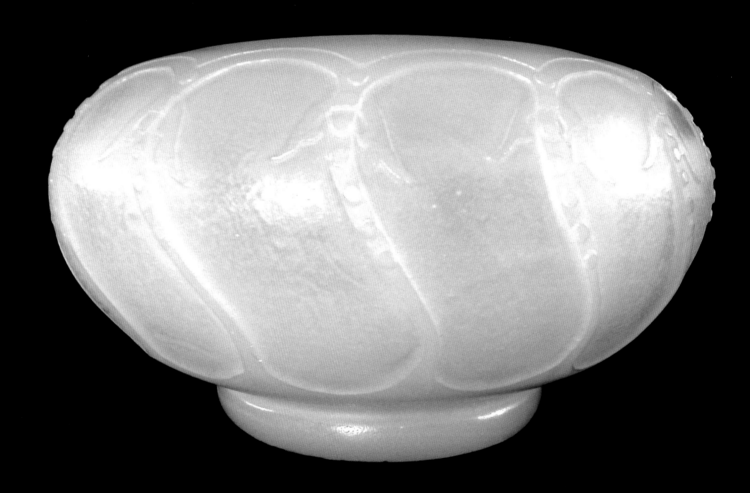

ALABASTER CUT CENTERBOWL IN CHIPPENDALE PATTERN
5 1/2 Inches High
Shape #6368

GREEN CUT TO ALABASTER VASE IN LOTUS PATTERN
9 1/2 Inches High
Shape #5000

(View of Two Panels)

MIRROR BLACK VASE CUT TO TURQUOISE IN FLAMBEAU PATTERN

12 Inches High
Shape #3273

The unusual and contrasting Black over Blue color combination demands attention. This pattern is unusual in that there are two slightly alternating panels. The pattern evokes a sense of ancient Egypt with one panel showing a bowl with flames and the alternating panel showing a bowl of fruit. This vase shows Mr. Carder's admiration for classic Egyptian design.

Grape Pattern
12 Inches High
Shape #6222
(left)

Cliftwood Pattern
10 1/2 Inches High
Shape #6272
(right)

MIRROR BLACK VASES CUT TO GREEN JADE

Mr. Carder's highly stylized designs for his acid cut backs represent some of the finest work ever done at Steuben. They were innovative, brightly colored and so attractive that they gained wide acceptance with those capable of affording them. The first step in creating an acid cut back vase is to blow the glass into the desired form. In the case of these vases, a gather of Green Jade was thinly cased in Mirror Black. Once cooled, the finished vase was sent to the cutting room. To create the complex Grape or Cliftwood pattern on these wonderful Steuben vases required three separate acid cuttings. Each cutting required precise alignment of a pattern on the vase. The areas which were to be left uncut were painted with beeswax and then the vase was subjected to a bath in hydrofluoric acid. This acid eats through glass, but beeswax is impervious to its effects. When the pattern has been etched deeply enough, the vase is removed from the acid bath. The residues of acid and beeswax are removed and the next pattern is painstakingly aligned as the process repeats for each part of the design. For example, when making the vase on the left, the first shallow cut created the veins within the leaves. The second deeper cut went through the black glass leaving a pattern of bunches of black grapes, curling leaves and a network of swirling vines against the lovely Green Jade. Interestingly, this cut satinized the green background leaving it in even sharper contrast against the shiny black, raised details of the pattern. The last cut created a tone on a tone network of scrolling geometric patterns to add texture and complexity to the finished vase. This was a very labor intensive process that put these acid cut backs out of reach for all but Steuben's affluent customers. Note, the more cuttings, the more costly the finished item. Today these acid cut pieces are among the most sought after of Steuben items with prices rising dramatically in recent years.

BLUE AURENE VASE CUT TO POMONA GREEN IN THE DEBUT PATTERN
8 Inches High
Shape #6882

The Art Deco style might be described as having dramatic color contrasts, boldly stylized geometric forms and dramatic silhouettes. Even complex designs in the Art Deco style give the appearance of elegant simplicity. Here Mr. Carder captures this spirit of the Art Deco movement in his Debut pattern vase. He begins with an unusual combination of Blue Aurene, infrequently used in acid etching, contrasted against a Pomona Green. Then he contrasts the angularity of the vase form and its similarly angular leaves against a flower whose petals are comprised of gently arched Blue Aurene forms.

CLUTHRA VASE OF POMONA GREEN CUT TO ROSE, SHADED TO BROWN IN THE BOOTHBAY PATTERN

14 Inches High
Shape #7007

The Boothbay vase (pictured above) and the Cliftwood Vase (on the next page) represent the pinnacle of Mr. Carder's mastery of the Art Deco style. It is a remarkable rethinking of the classic leaf and vine motif. The zig zagging vines and angular leaves are Art Deco at its very best. The contrast between the strong lines of the pattern and the soft curves of the vases further serves to emphasize the dramatic Boothbay and Cliftwood patterns. The complexity of the glass itself perfectly compliments and amplifies the drama of this vase. The Pomona Green outer layer cased over Rose Cluthra shading to a darker color at the base are in perfect harmony.

**POMONA GREEN VASE CUT TO ROSE CLUTHRA
IN THE CLIFTWOOD PATTERN**
14 Inches High
Shape #7000

BLUE AURENE VASE CUT TO MIRROR BLACK IN THE GRAPE PATTERN
10 3/4 Inches High
Shape #2683

The Shape #2683 vase is quite often found in Blue Aurene or Gold Aurene without decoration. This flowing shape is a Steuben standard and has great desirability and popularity. This vase is particularly strong and dramatic due to its imposing size coupled with a relatively simple etched pattern.

GOLD AURENE VASE CUT TO BLACK IN THE NORFOLK PATTERN
8 1/2 Inches High
Shape #2683

The striking contrast between the brilliant Gold Aurene and mirrored finished black glass adds dimension and vibrancy to the complex beauty of the Norfolk pattern. This classic shape is reminiscent of an ancient Greek Amphora.

GOLD AURENE VASE CUT TO BLACK, WHICH WAS THEN CUT TO A PEBBLED BACKGROUND IN THE THISTLE PATTERN
7 3/4 Inches High
Shape #6078

Both the Norfolk pattern vase on the prior page and this Thistle pattern vase are Gold Aurene over Black. However, by the use of pebbling in this Thistle pattern vase, quite a different effect is produced.

BLUE AURENE VASE CUT TO YELLOW JADE
IN A VARIANT OF THE AZALEA PATTERN
12 1/2 Inches High
Shape #8413

The strong Yellow Jade color causes the thin Blue Aurene layer to often look like Gold Aurene as shown at the top of this vase.

Colombo Pattern
10 Inches High
Shape #7095

Majestic Pattern
8 1/4 Inches High
Shape #6227

GREEN JADE VASES CUT TO YELLOW JADE

It's reported that Mr. Carder so disliked Yellow Jade that he refused to acknowledge the few pieces presented to him for authentication. Therefore, little Yellow Jade glass is attributed to Steuben, leading to a greater degree of rarity when found. These five pieces are quite different visually and all are pleasing to the eye. The use of Brown, Blue Aurene and Pomona Green casing each create quite wonderful and varied finished works.

BROWN CUT TO YELLOW JADE SPRINGTIME PATTERN (WITH MALLARD)
10 Inches High
Shape #6272

Raindrops are etched on yellow glass. The Mallard color is different from the leaves, created by a different thickness in the etching.

YELLOW JADE CUT CHRYSANTHEMUM PATTERN
6 1/8 Inches High
Shape #6199

PLUM JADE BOWL IN CHANG PATTERN
8 Inches High, 9 1/2 Inches Wide
Shape #6112

Plum Jade utilizes three layers of glass. In this vase, the outer layer of amethyst glass is acid etched to expose the inner core of alabaster glass. The background is given a second acid cutting to give it a rough texture. The richness of the Plum Jade is reminiscent of Peking Glass and was commonly acid cut into Chinese patterns.

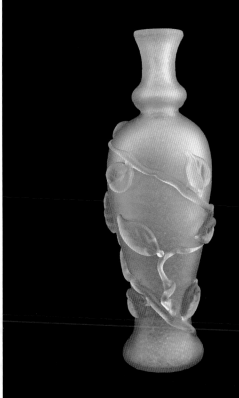

CINNAMON VASE WITH APPLIED SCULPTURAL VINE AND ACID CUT LEAVES
11 1/2 Inches High
Shape #8471

Steuben referred to this beautiful style of decoration as sculptured. The applied leaves have acid cut veins. Sometimes a few Art Deco acid cut back flowers can be found dancing on the surface. Sculptured vases and lamp shafts can also be found in Quartz Glass. These pieces are an imitation of the mineral Quartz and are distinguished by internal crackling on Cintra Glass.

ROSE QUARTZ FOOTED BOWL WITH SCULPTURAL AND ACID ETCHED DECORATION

7 Inches High
Shape #6856

The Quartz bowl doesn't appear, at first blush, to be acid etched. Its etched pattern is subtle and only one characteristic of the many techniques employed. This bowl has external colorless sculpturing.

The Rose Quartz bowl has feet that are added to the piece at the fire, but are separate from the subtle etched floral pattern in the piece. The Rose colored glass is known by factory records as Rose Quartz, following a theme of nature in both substance and the flower appliqué. The Rose glass itself contains blue flecks and is internally crackled. The collection of the many design skills and glass blowing techniques contained in the Rose Quartz bowl serve to show off the best of design, workmanship, and quality of Mr. Carder and his skilled glass blower team.

MIRROR BLACK VASE CUT TO ALABASTER IN NEDRA PATTERN
7 Inches High
Shape #6078

ROSALINE GINGER JAR CUT TO ALABASTER
Glass 9 1/2 Inches High, Mounts 14 1/2 Inches High
Shape #5000

This pattern is unidentified. The mounts, made of wood and gesso, are original to the vase. Mounts of this type were commonly found on exhibition pieces and it could be speculated that this vase was made for that purpose. The cut pattern is an unusual mix of styles which also strengthens the likelihood that this stunning vase was made for a special exhibition.

ROSALINE CUT TO ALABASTER IN THE MATZU PATTERN
7 Inches High
Shape #6078

GREEN JADE VASE CUT TO ALABASTER IN PEONY PATTERN
9 1/2 Inches High
Shape #7391

GREEN JADE CENTERPIECE BOWL CUT TO ALABASTER
IN THE CHINESE PATTERN
4 1/2 Inches High, 12 3/4 Inches Wide
Shape #3103

GREEN JADE VASE CUT TO ALABASTER IN SHERWOOD PATTERN
7 Inches High
Shape #6078

GREEN VASE CUT TO ALABASTER IN GRETA PATTERN
6 1/4 Inches High
Shape #7444

ROSALINE VASE CUT TO ALABASTER IN MAYFAIR PATTERN

12 Inches High

Shape #7442

MIRROR BLACK LAMP BASE CUT TO GREEN JADE IN PAGODA PATTERN
12 Inches High
Shape #6097

The Pagoda Pattern is a Chinese village scene of an arched bridge and people. What might appear to be a smudge in the decoration are clouds.

GREEN JADE LAMP BASE CUT TO ALABASTER IN PAGODA PATTERN
12 Inches High
Shape #6375

Note that the previous lamp is the identical pattern. However, with a combination of different shape and dominant color, the effect is totally different.

GOLD AURENE LAMP BASE CUT TO GREEN JADE IN MODERNE PATTERN
12 3/4 Inches High
Shape #2144

GOLD AURENE VASE CUT TO ALABASTER IN VINES PATTERN
11 5/8 Inches High
Shape #6390

Exotics

While this collection consists of a good number of rarities, I have selected a few particularly unique designs or techniques that could well be identified as "Exotics". Of these, Intarsia and Cire Perdue are Mr. Carder's most significant contributions.

GODDESS "ELECTRA"
9 1/4 Inches High
CIRE PERDUE

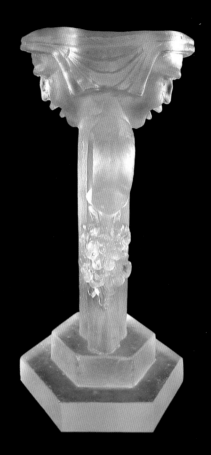

In 1932 Mr. Carder, at age 69, was relieved from his position as manager of Steuben and named Art Director of the Corning Glass Works. He moved to a small studio within the factory and was given the opportunity to experiment. This began his studio period. Some of his finest work came out of this time until his retirement in 1959, at age 96. During this period Mr. Carder drew from his storehouse of knowledge to recreate and perfect the Roman process of cast glass, often referred to as the "Lost Wax Process". A simpler cast glass had been achieved in the late 1800s by René Lalique and was greatly admired by Mr. Carder. The process allowed for intricate designs in glass, a process normally applied to metals not glass. Mr. Carder applied his intellectual curiosity through extensive experimentation with mold materials and techniques to harness the difficult *Cire Perdue* cast process that could withstand temperatures and stresses of casting without small parts of the mold breaking or glass breaking away from the object. The complex eight step process was painstakingly executed and carried out by Mr. Carder in his studio. It began with a clay model from which a plaster casting was made. The casting was used to make a wax model of the subject and ultimately through a series of steps to a finished figure in clear frosted crystal. Incredibly detailed and complex subjects could include almost anything commonly found in metal sculptures. Production was limited to either a single example or a scant few from each plaster mold. Quality was diminished with each subsequent casting. Many of the finished products were given to friends or museums.

The above double candlestick, shown from two different angles, is unique in that it was commissioned in 1939 as part of a pair of candlesticks used for a dinner honoring the sixtieth anniversary of the invention of the light bulb by Thomas Alva Edison. At the conclusion of the evening one of the pair of candlesticks disappeared and has not since resurfaced. This remaining candlestick was returned to Mr. Carder. This candlestick of the Greek

TYRIAN VASE WITH GOLD AURENE HEART
AND TRAILED LEAF-AND-VINE DECORATION
4 3/4 Inches High
Shape #2784

TYRIAN VASE

In 1916 Mr. Carder introduced a new technique which he called Tyrian. He patterned it after the colorful fabrics produced in ancient Tyre. Tyrian is a heat reactive glass that begins as green in color. During production the glass is reheated at the top of the object causing it to take on a purple tone which then shades back to the green in the unheated portions. The greater the exposure to the reheating, the more pronounced the color shift.

Each piece has its own unique and typically elegant shape and most are marked "TYRIAN". The difficulty in achieving the properly shaded coloration accounts for its limited production, making each piece of Tyrian an extreme rarity. Most objects have Gold Aurene trailed leaf-and-vine decoration marvered into the iridescent body.

TUMBLER
4 1/4 Inches High
Shape #6358

TOOTHBRUSH HOLDER
4 1/2 Inches High
Shape #6767

ROUGE FLAMBÉ WITH RANDOM REEDING

Signed "Fred'k Carder"

Frederick Carder had long been fascinated by a centuries old Chinese porcelain glaze called Sang de Boeuf (ox blood). This intense red glaze was not for the masses and today can be very expensive. Mr. Carder set out to translate the color and intensity of this glaze into glass. Although Mr. Carder was a consummate chemist having created over one hundred glass colors during his long career, this color eluded him. It varied widely in the shade of red; and worse, the glass was proven very delicate to internal strains that would cause many pieces to fracture during the annealing (cool down) process.

Rouge Flambé, as it was named, is a color for which Mr. Carder was justly proud. Its fragile nature, combined with the difficulty in controlling the finished color, meant that very few pieces were made. Mr. Carder stated that only about one hundred items were ever made in this elusive color. The best pieces have a rich, opaque, tomato red color that truly has the look of porcelain. The color ranged from a darker red to a coral.

Mr. Carder kept the shapes pretty simple so as not to distract anyone's attention from the beautiful red color. It has been reported that this color was first developed in 1916, but an ad for it appears in a 1926 publication of *House and Garden* magazine. Given the extremely limited production, it is not likely that it remained in production for ten years.

This bathroom set consists of a toothbrush holder and a tumbler. It is likely that there were other pieces in this set. These are currently the only two known pieces to be decorated with random Rouge Flambé reeding. A few pieces were also decorated with Gold Aurene leaves and vines. The color attained on these two pieces is excellent.

The toothbrush holder has a production era "Fred'k Carder" signature. It has been long thought that Mr. Carder only used this signature on Steuben's Intarsia glass. As with Intarsia, Mr. Carder's signature is engraved prominently on the side of the object proudly proclaiming its importance. Paul Gardner reported this to be a facsimile signature, but in an interview, Mr. Carder said that he personally signed each piece of Intarsia and presumably this toothbrush holder as well.

(Front signed side)   (Opposite side)

INTARSIA VASE WITH BLACK FLORAL
AND VINE DESIGN IN CRYSTAL WITH BLACK FOOT
9 1/4 Inches High

Intarsia, taken from the Italian word for "inlay", is Mr. Carder's crowning artistic achievement. He considered this the most technically difficult of his pieces. Mr. Carder pushed the limits of Steuben's most capable gaffer, Johnny Jansson, who was the only gaffer he trusted to make the most difficult pieces, including all of the Intarsia. Even though some seventy years have passed, Intarsia has yet to be duplicated by any other glass house. Mr. Carder estimated there were only 35-40 pieces of Intarsia produced at Steuben. Today, most are in museum collections.

An approximately 3 inch by 1 1/2 inch crystal of hot glass is covered by a thin layer of blue, black, green or amethyst glass and then cooled. A floral or foliate design is etched through the colored casing. The etched glass is slowly reheated and cased with yet another layer of clear crystal, which is then carefully blown out into a 6 to 8 inch vase or object, so as not to distort but to elongate and enlarge the design to create beautiful effects.

Intarsia presents the viewer with the illusion that the design is ethereal, floating free within the glass. This vase, echoing the shape of an unrecorded flower blossom, barely contains a virtual explosion of stylized blossoms and vines blowing in a gentle breeze and growing larger as they attain their full height near the rim. This vase with its shapely and elegant form is reminiscent of the earlier Art Nouveau period.

As an affirmation of the importance of his Intarsia creations, nearly all pieces were embellished with the flourish of his unique personally signed, "Fred'k Carder". This copper engraved signature isn't the typical identification on the bottom of the piece, but rather appears boldly emblazoned on the side of the piece, much as a painter would sign his canvas.

CENTERPIECE BOWL WITH SCULPTURED FIGURES
20 Inches High
Shape #6497

FLOWER FROG WITH KNEELING NUDE ORNAMENT
7 Inches High
Shape #6495

The diving lady figural is a table centerpiece assembled solely from five glass components.

Very few pieces of Steuben Glass are so rare that they would qualify as being virtually unobtainable. This centerpiece bowl is one such piece. The rich brown of the base was given the name Cairn Gorm and is among Steuben's rarest colors. The base is faceted on six sides. Both the Bristol Yellow bowl and the three figural crystal supports are acid finished to allow a soft glow and provide a textural contrast to the glossy base.

For additional interest, the yellow bowl has an inclusion of controlled bubbles. The diving nude figures were an off the shelf component more commonly found as individual ornaments mounted in a cut crystal holder. This was designed as a luxury item as evidenced by its 1926 wholesale price of $100.

A clear crystal flower frog and kneeling nude figurine are shown to suggest a use for flower frogs.

Fn. A similar centerpiece in green is part of the collection of the Rockwell Museum pictured at Fig. 4.149, p. 104 of <u>Frederick Carder and Steuben Glass</u> by Thomas P. Dimitroff. The Museum version does not have bubbles.

PINK AND BLUE OR VERRE VASE WITH APPLIED MIRROR BLACK RIM
10 Inches High
Shape #3218

The addition of vertical stripes to Cintra adds a focal point that is somewhat unusual and is called Controlled Cintra or Or Verre. Keeping the stripes vertical, separate and straight required a skilled gaffer, accounting for the rarity of Or Verre today.

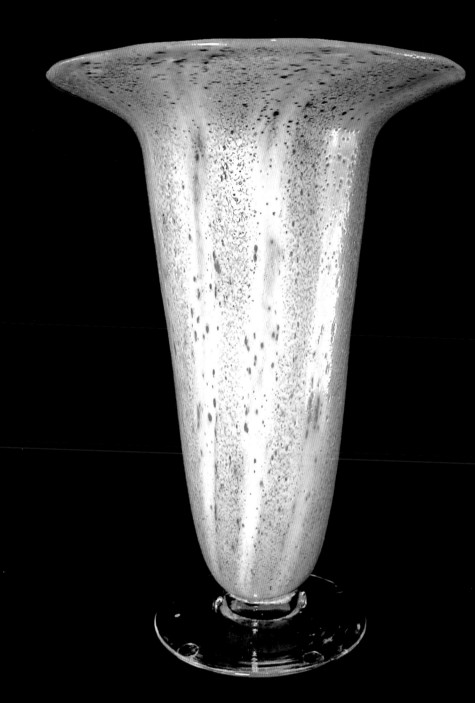

GREEN AND WHITE LACE GLASS VASE WITH CLEAR CRYSTAL FOOT
10 1/4 Inches High
Shape #7169

Lace glass is one of the more unusual and rarest techniques ever made at Steuben. It was a late period creation; and the small number of shapes produced reflected that, with forms that are very clean and modern looking. Like Cintra, the colors were derived from powdered and finely crushed glass. The encased bubbles are somewhat like those found in Cluthra although they lack Cluthra's thick outer casing of clear glass. This retarded the ability of the bubbles to grow larger. A collector would be very lucky to ever find an example of Lace Glass in the marketplace.

MOSS AGATE LAMP
11 Inches High Glass
Shape #6098

Glassmakers for centuries have attempted to capture the beauty of agate, chalcedony, marble and other stones in their glass. While some of these efforts have met with a limited measure of success and have produced some very interesting glass, Mr. Carder's work on Moss Agate is seminal. In this technique he accurately captured the beauty and incredible complexity of the semi-precious stone.

Achieving this technique required the incorporation of skills developed through the production of many of Moss Agate's predecessors at Steuben. Moss Agate is most likely the only glass Mr. Carder attempted that needed four different layers of glass. A parison of Topaz glass was rolled on a marver of powdered glass in warm tones and white. After that was marvered into the Topaz, the parison was then rolled in coarsely crushed glass that included some fairly large chunks. Colors included Amethyst, Blue, Green and Red. Upon reheating, the larger chunks were hooked or pulled into shapes simulating the veining found in natural agates. The mass was again used to pick up mica flecks before casing it in an outer layer of colored or clear glass. Colors used were Topaz, Celeste Blue or Amethyst. An inclusion of very fine bubbles may be seen floating within this casing.

After blowing the gather into its final form, water was poured into the form, swirled and quickly poured out. This was a critical step that could fracture the glass. If all went well, it would create a network of barely perceptible cracks, mirroring that found in nature.

Moss Agate was one of the most complex, difficult and expensive techniques ever produced at Steuben. Today, it is an extreme rarity, seldom found in any form other than lamps. Tan and Brown are the more common colors, with Blue and Amethyst being almost unobtainable.

FLORENTIA CENTERPIECE BOWL
AN INTERNALLY DECORATED BOWL WITH A PINK (CINNAMON) JADE FIVE PETAL FLOWER, SILVER MICA FLECKS AND MATTE FINISH

14 Inch Diameter
3 Inches High
Shape #6784

Florentia is found with a Green or Pink (Cinnamon) flower. A few pieces of Florentia were made with a green flower on a yellow background. Florentia is rare. This center bowl is particularly seductive. The 14" diameter provides an unusually large, charger like, shallow vessel that spreads open its five-petal delicate flower. When viewed from above, the flower may be seen in its full beauty as if it had opened itself to the sun for the world to enjoy and is now floating in a shimmering pool of water. The entrapped mica flecks sparkle like sunlight on the water.

GREEN FLORENTIA VASE
12 inches High
Shape 6731

The five petal flower decoration is made of powdered glass particles cased between two layers of clear glass with cased mica floating flecks. The outer surface is given an acid bath which leaves it pebbled and frosted.

Perfumes

PERFUME BOTTLES
WITH FLORAL STOPPERS (from left)
MIRROR BLACK AND TURQUOISE,
GOLD AURENE AND CINNAMON,
AND BLUE AURENE AND TURQUOISE
7 Inches High
Shape #3425

Mr. Carder designed a wonderful and stylish selection of colognes and perfume bottles. They were made in almost every color imaginable with a wide variety of decorations and finishes. Brightly colored flowers, like these, were used in moderation at Steuben. They will most likely be found on perfume bottles, but may also turn up as finials on covered pieces or as ornamentation on a basket or candelabrum. These flowers are reproduced in a naturalistic manner and beautifully colored with the use of cased glass. The long black stamens add the perfect touch to these fanciful stoppers. Individually or in groups, these bottles are sure to bring a bit of sunshine and the outdoors to a lady's vanity table. Other embellishments such as the applied Rigaree handles on the Gold Aurene Bottle add an air of grace and elegance.

GOLD AURENE AND CINNAMON
PERFUME BOTTLE
6 1/4 Inches High
Shape #3427

FLEMISH BLUE PERFUME
7 Inches High
Shape #3174

**RIBBED AMETHYST PERFUME
WITH CLEAR CRYSTAL THREE PILLAR CROWN STOPPER**
4 1/2 Inches High
Shape #3093

These paperweight ball connectors were used sparingly at Steuben. They were principally used in these fanciful, tall perfume bottles, but may also be found in covered boxes and compotes. The internal decoration is always the same and is comprised of swirled orange latticino, bubbles and mica within a clear glass matrix. These stunning paperweight pieces are scarce and are a worthy addition to any collection.

SELENIUM RUBY PERFUME WITH ROPE STOPPER AND PAPERWEIGHT CONNECTOR
12 1/2 Inches High
Shape #6024

CLEAR PERFUME WITH PINK CINTRA RIM AND FLOWERED STOPPER
4 1/2 Inches High
Shape #3404

GOLD AURENE BELL SHAPED PERFUME
6 Inches High
Shape #1818

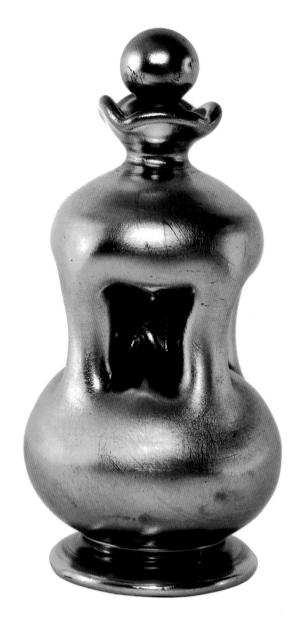

BLUE AURENE PINCHED PERFUME WITH BALL STOPPER
3 1/8 Inches High
Shape # 2834

MINIATURE PERFUME BOTTLES

Whether it is in the field of music, theater, film, fine arts or crafts, it takes a real master to take something old and make it new again, fresh and vital. Such is the case with this charming little perfume. Mr. Carder started with a 150 year old design for a British whiskey decanter and scaled it down to almost miniature size, added a ruffled rim, a foot and the lustrous iridescence of Steuben's Blue Aurene to create this delightful confection. Mr. Carder successfully adapted that concept into a highly regarded line which included a perfume, an atomizer, vases, bowls and even a decanter set. Here it is in all its shades of blues, purples and greens. The pinches and folds lend themselves particularly well to an Aurene treatment. The complex shape creates areas of brilliant highlights and dark mystery. I do not believe that this form was ever adapted to any other makers' iridized glass lines, making these Carder forms unique in the world.

BLUE AURENE
3 1/4 Inches High
Shape #2835

GOLD AURENE
4 1/4 Inches High
Shape #2758

BLUE AURENE
3 3/4 Inches High
Shape #2833

**BRISTOL
YELLOW
PERFUME**

4 1/4 Inches High
Shape #6233

**OPALESCENT
COLOGNE
WITH LIGHT JADE
BLUE STOPPER**

4 1/4 Inches High
Shape #3271

**VERRE DE SOIE
BOTTLE WITH
FLEMISH BLUE
STOPPER**

3 1/2 Inches High
Shape #2835

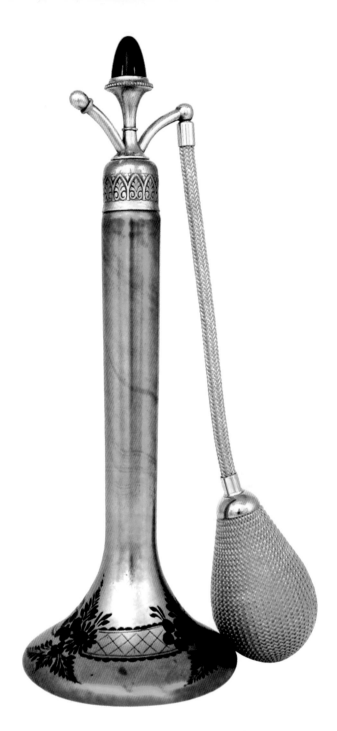

DEVILBISS GOLD & BLUE AURENE PERFUME ATOMIZERS
WITH ENGRAVED BASES
12 Inches High
Shape #6407

Many glassmakers worldwide contracted with Devilbiss to provide glass blanks that would be turned into atomizers and perfumes. These tall atomizers are usually found with the engraving and unique atomizer parts that include the stately, glass acorn finials seen here. Some confusion may exist as other glassmakers supplied Devilbiss with some of the same shapes as Steuben provided. The Gold and Blue atomizers were exclusively Steuben glass.

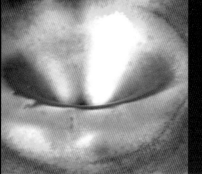

Jack-in-the-Pulpit

Today we consider Jack-in-the-Pulpit vases to be the quintessential examples of the Art Nouveau period. Steuben's Jack-in-the-Pulpits are early in the history of the company, few in number, and today are highly desirable and scarce. The outsized, highly stylized and undulating flower blossom commands attention. A wonderful example is shown center below, and on the next page, with its broad 6 3/4 inch sensual and exotic flower, and with its rings of fiery red iridescent stretched Gold Aurene on the blossom. This stretching is intentional, and found particularly on flaring rims and discs. It is caused by the stretching of the molten glass under the metallic coating. Shape #130 on the next page left, has a brilliant platinum iridescent flower blossom. The variances in color are results of differences in reducing flame heat treatment as the piece undergoes chemical sprays in the making.

8 3/4 Inches High
Shape #130

10 3/4 Inches High
Shape #751
"HAVILAND"

6 Inches High
Shape #2699

JACK-IN-THE-PULPIT VASES

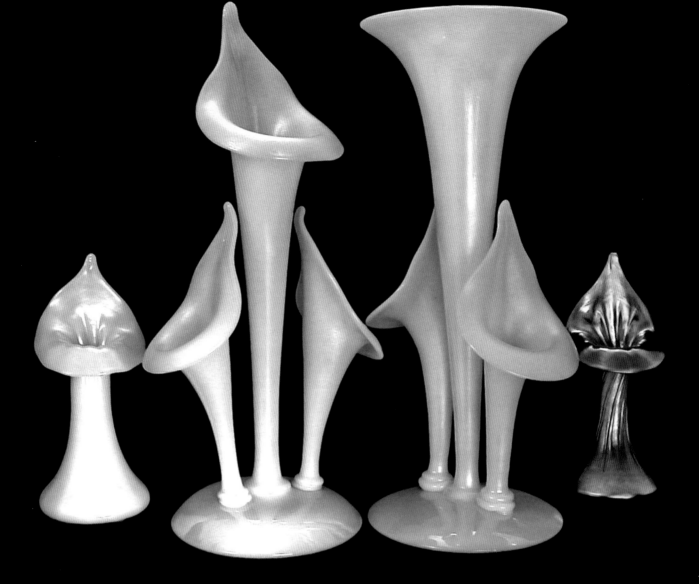

6 3/4 Inches High
Shape #7560

12 1/4 Inches High
Shape #7595

12 Inches High
Shape #7566

6 3/4 Inches High
Shape #7560

LILY VASES

Lily vases are post World War I Art Deco period pieces, yet retain a flower form that carries over from the Art Nouveau period. The flowers are small and tightly formed. The rims roll downward and the forms are extremely stylized in the Deco mode. Ivrene is a lightly iridescent, soft snow white opaque glass. This art form lends itself well to the stark severity of Lily vases, and that is why most are made in Ivrene. Lily vases are unique and very separate from Jack-in-the-Pulpit vases and should be given their own individual due. The #7560 vase in Ivrene at the far left is represented again in Gold Aurene on the far right. The two vases in the center are variants of each other, varying in the use of a tall lily or trumpet as the center column. Lily vases are frequently found mislabeled as Jack-in-the-Pulpit vases.

Colored and Clear Crystals

Mr. Carder's incorporation of design elements found in Venetian glass was so ever-present at Steuben to render much of his colored crystal art glass synonymous with Venetian glass. It was a theme from which he rarely strayed. This is not to say that the colored crystal produced under Mr. Carder's direction was imitative. In fact, it was far from that.

Nowhere in Steuben's rich history was Mr. Carder more creative than with his colored crystal glassware. He created a vast array of colors and deftly combined them through the use of appliqués, shading and contrasting stem elements on candlesticks, compotes and the like. Rather than rely on the Venetians' use of internal decorations such as latticino, filligrano, gold powders and the like, Mr. Carder let his beautiful forms and tasteful embellishments speak for themselves. Speak they did to generations of art glass buyers and they still speak to us through their classic elegance and beauty.

On these pages, you will find many Venetian style elements adapted to Steuben's colorful crystal. Look for appliqués like prunts, reeding, ring handles, and a myriad of fanciful finials. Study the way stems are elegantly constructed and pieced together with blown elements that are hollow and exquisitely thin. Note the rims that frequently incorporate a thin edge of glass being rolled under and see how optic molds were used to create patterns within the glass.

Mr. Carder borrowed all these stylistic elements from the Venetians, but the glass he created was wholly new, fresh and all Steuben. One hundred years later, it is safe to state unequivocally that Mr. Carder's Steuben glass is timeless and always current.

AMETHYST SILVERINA VASE
12 Inches High
Shape #7008

Diamond air-trapped glass with mica flecks.

CLEAR CRYSTAL VANITY JAR WITH MIRROR BLACK REEDING AND FACETED LID

8 1/2 Inches High

Shape #6733

F. CARDER POST PRODUCTION SIGNATURE

This outsized jar is part of a design for a vanity set that had many matching components that could be mixed or matched. This jar, perhaps used for cotton puffs or bath salts, is more commonly found in a six inch size designated for cold cream.

AMBER & CELESTE BLUE VASE WITH PRUNTS, LATTICE WORK COVER & CROWN FINIAL

13 1/2 Inches High
Shape Variant of #3109

AMETHYST
10 Inches High
Shape #2909

CARDINAL RED
8 Inches High
Shape #2909

MOSS GREEN
10 Inches High
Shape #2909

RING HANDLED VASES

SELENIUM RUBY RING HANDLED CENTERPIECE BOWL
8 3/4 Inches High
Shape # 2942

This imposing table centerpiece captures many of the style elements found in Venetian glass. The ring handles were a complex and eye catching embellishment that Mr. Carder seemed to favor. The rolled rim wafers and hollow knop connector are typical of many devices used by Steuben for their Venetian pieces. The beauty of this centerpiece bowl is found in its timeless style and intensely deep red color.

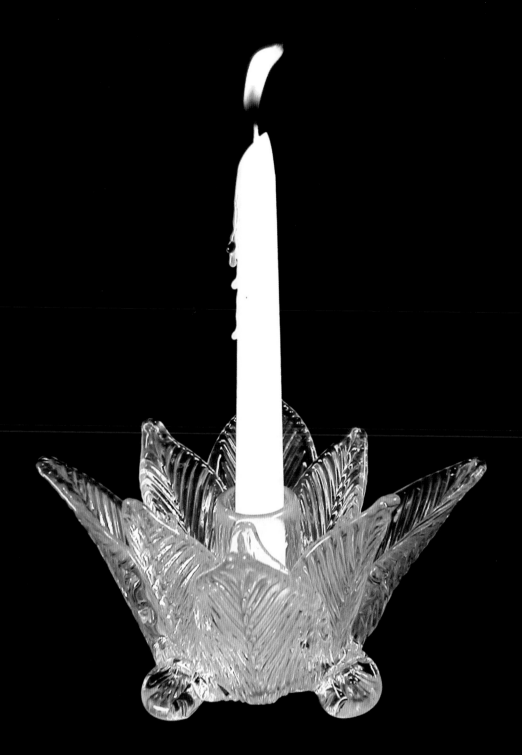

CRYSTAL CANDLEHOLDER WITH APPLIED LEAVES AND FEET
3 1/2 Inches High
Shape #7637

The veining in these leaves is achieved with a pincered tool that when closed around the glass gather impresses the veining. Each veined leaf must then be formed and shaped by hand at the fire which accounts for their variation from one another.

CRYSTAL GOBLETS WITH BLACK RANDOM REEDING AND PRUNTS
6 1/2 Inches High to 8 Inches High
Shape #6603

Threads of molten, colored glass, applied randomly to the body of an object, are referred to as a "reeded" decoration. Reeding was a commonly used technique employed on Steuben's Venetian art glass. It was relatively quick and easy, but yielded some dramatic results as evidenced by these gorgeous goblets.

CELESTE BLUE BOWL WITH DIAMOND QUILTED OPTIC PATTERN AND TOPAZ REEDING
4 1/2 Inches High
Shape #6778

CRYSTAL BOWL WITH APPLIED GOLD RUBY BANDS, RIMS, PRUNTS AND MACHINE THREADING
5 3/4 Inches High
Shape #3369

POMONA GREEN BOWL WITH AN OPTIC RIB PATTERN, TOPAZ PEDESTAL FOOT WITH ROLLED RIM, MICA INCLUSIONS AND HOOKED PRUNTS

7 Inches High
Shape #6046

The Venetian glassmakers have encased gold dust in their glassware for centuries. Mr. Carder preferred a larger mica fleck. Examples with mica fleck inclusions are scarce.

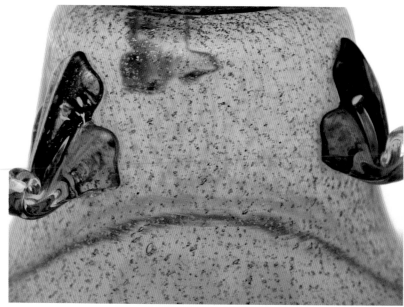

TOPAZ COMPOTE WITH APPLIED CELESTE BLUE BANDS, RIM AND FLOWER PRUNTS

8 3/4 Inches High
Shape #3372

TOPAZ BOWL PINCHED PEDESTAL BASE
AND APPLIED FLEMISH BLUE RIM AND PRUNTS

5 Inches High
Shape #3080

This fanciful shape, with its pinched glass column, has four hollow tubes that could be used as an aid to flower arranging. The shape has become identified as an atomic cloud shape owing to its similarity to that now familiar aftermath of an atomic bomb blast.

SELENIUM RUBY PUFF BOX WITH OPTIC RIBS AND FLOWER FINIAL
4 1/4 Inches High
Shape #6158

Very few of these internally decorated flower finials have been found. They represent an unopened flower bud and include tiny bubbles, mica flecks and latticino bands of cinnamon colored glass.

FLORAL FINIAL

**AMETHYST COMPOTE WITH OPTIC RIBS, HOLLOW STEM
AND CONTRASTING CRYSTAL WAFERS**
10 Inches High
Shape #6868

ROYAL PURPLE VASE WITH EIGHT APPLIED FLINT WHITE STRIPES
10 Inches High
Shape #1901

The factory records identify this color as "RP." While many unidentified shades of purple were used at Steuben, this one is probably Royal Purple.

**TULIP CANDLEHOLDER WITH CELESTE BLUE FLOWER AND LEAF BASE
DARK TOPAZ TWISTED THORNY STEM**

12 Inches High

Shape #6058

CRACKLED TOPAZ VASE WITH POMONA GREEN LION HEAD PRUNTS

9 1/2 Inches High
Shape #6199

This vase combines several elements rarely used at Steuben. The lion head prunts are taken directly from a similar Venetian style prunt. Mr. Carder designed very little crackled glass. Lastly, this is a mold blown vase wholly deriving its shape from a mold. The resulting vase was cut off at the top. The rim was chamfered in and out and polished to a high gloss. Owing to the fact that it was mold blown, the glass is much thicker than is commonly found in Steuben's free blown crystal pieces.

SPANISH GREEN LATTICE WORK BASKET
WITH APPLIED HANDLES AND BERRY PRUNTS
4 3/4 Inches High
Shape #644

While referred to as lattice work, woven or basket weave, this effect requires no weaving of the glass canes. Rather, it is built up in layers by zig zagging the canes and attaching each new layer to the apex points of the previous layer. This may have been done around a metal or wooden form to provide shape. Whether around a form or freehand, this was a difficult thing to do while working with molten glass without having the final form collapse or sag. This basket came with a separate clear glass liner that slipped inside and could hold water.

AMBER AND FLEMISH BLUE 1/2 PINT DECANTER WITH CROWN STOPPER AND THREE CORDIALS

9 Inches High
Cups 2 1/2 Inches High
Shape #2931

This decanter was available in the 1/2 pint or 1 pint size.

CLEAR CRYSTAL CREAMER AND SUGAR WITH CELESTE BLUE MATSU-NO-KE DECORATION

Creamer 4 Inches High
Sugar 3 1/4 Inches High
Shape #3335

Matsu-No-Ke is a clear crystal with applied, transparent, colored décor and handles. The appliqué has the appearance of veined oval cactuses. This technique had been used by Mr. Carder during his days in England, while he was at Stevens & Williams in the 1880s. Apparently Stevens & Williams, and later Steuben, applied for patents on this technique.

**TOPAZ CRACKLED GLASS
LAMP WITH FANCY GREEN
CINTRA HANDLES
AND BRASS MOUNTS**
Glass 11 Inches High
Lamp totals 26 Inches High
Shape #6550

Jade and Other Translucent Colors

MOLD BLOWN GREEN JADE PANELED VASE
4 1/2 Inches High
Shape #6415
Mirrors a Peking Glass Shape

DARK BLUE JADE VASE WITH OPTIC RIBS
11 Inches High
Shape #7437

Mr. Carder attempted to translate the many brilliant jade colors found in nature to his Steuben glass. This rich cobalt blue was simply named Dark Blue Jade. Like all of the jade glassware produced at Steuben, this vase has a rich translucent quality which mimics its mineral namesake. Items in Dark Blue Jade are often found with an optic pattern of vertical ribs. This vase was blown into a sixteen rib optic mold and then fashioned into its final form.

COVERED IVORY PUFF BOX WITH MIRROR BLACK PEAR FINIAL
6 Inches High
Shape #2910

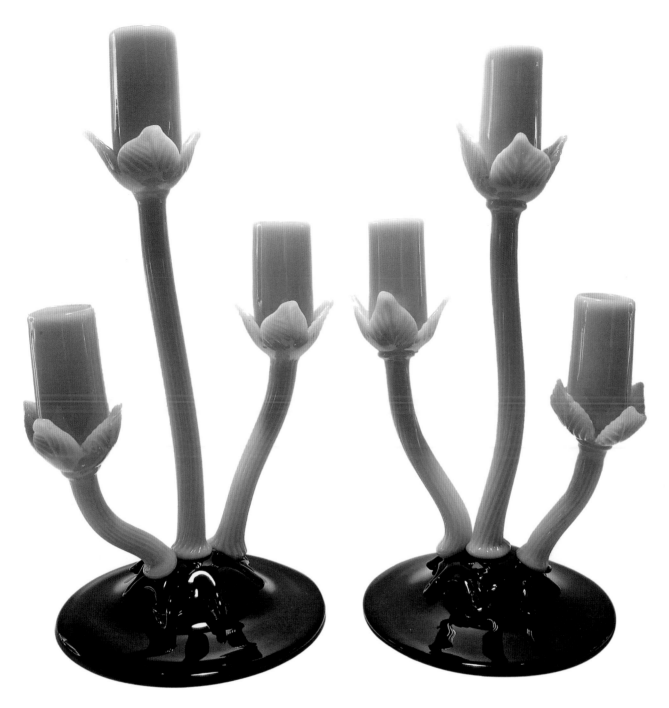

PAIR OF IVORY FLOWERS AND STEMS ON A MIRROR BLACK BASE
11 Inches High
Shape #7317

Candlesticks and candelabrum were a wonderful opportunity for Mr. Carder to express his creativity. These candelabra are among the scarcer and most coveted of these designs.

IVORY CHARGER WITH APPLIED MIRROR BLACK RIM
17 Inches Diameter
Shape #3187

LIGHT BLUE JADE PUFF BOX
WITH FLINT WHITE FINIAL
4 1/2 Inches High

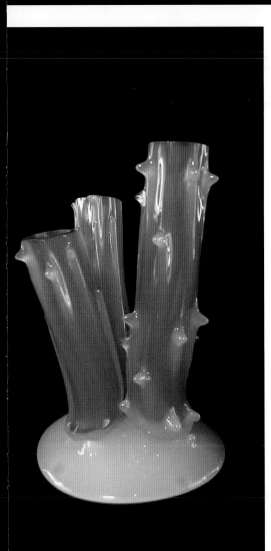

ROSALINE BUD VASE
WITH ALABASTER
FOOT AND PULLED
THORN DECORATION
(left)

OPAQUE MIRROR
BLACK TRIPLE BUD
VASE WITH PULLED
THORN DECORATION
(right)

6 Inches High
Shape #2744

These popular vases came in many sizes, numbers of stumps and a wild profusion of colors. They are actually one of the designs that Mr. Carder brought with him from Stevens & Williams and date to Victorian England. This design is known by many names, including Three Prong, Rustic, Stump Vase and Thorn Vase.

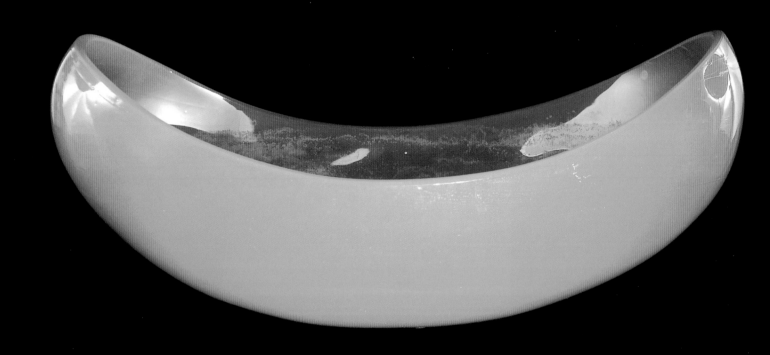

JADE GREEN CANOE CENTERPIECE BOWL
20 Inches Long
Shape #6515

This shape was dubbed a canoe bowl by Steuben. Other glassmakers produced similarly shaped bowls that are referred to as banana boats. This striking bowl is among the larger and heavier pieces attempted at Steuben. Its sheer mass must have made working with it difficult for the gaffer and his shop.

IVORY FIVE-PRONG VASE
9 1/2 Inches High
Shape #6968

Prong vases were a recurring theme at Steuben. Prongs were made in many different shapes and each prong design came in several different incarnations ranging from a single prong to as many as six, varying in size and placement on its foot. Many colors and combinations were used creating an infinite variety. Steuben's prong vases may also be found in shaded Cluthra colors and Aurenes. Around 1931 a colored crystal prong vase was briefly produced with a diamond quilted optic pattern in the prongs.

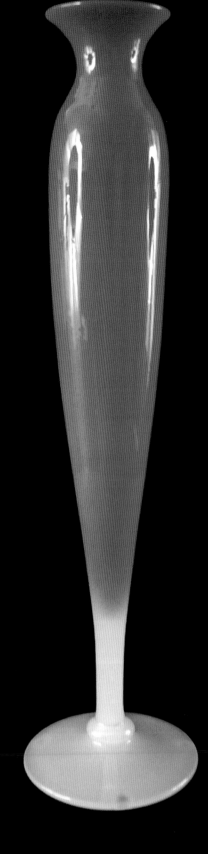

ROSALINE VASE SHADED TO ALABASTER

18 Inches High

Shape #775

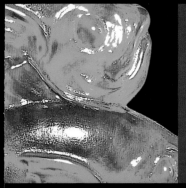

Table Decorations

Mr. Carder had a real talent for sculpture. His ability to translate a two dimensional drawing into a three dimensional object propelled him to create some magnificent figurals and plaques for Steuben. Sculpture is also the artistic endeavor that captured his imagination for the last thirty years of his life. This was his studio period at Steuben in which he created Cire Perdue and Diatreta. During this period he personally created every single piece as well as the process of casting the glass into a finished object.

For an artist of Mr. Carder's caliber, it must have been the most gratifying way possible to spend the closing years of his long life.

INTAGLIO CARVED AND MOLDED PLAQUE OF A YOUNG GLADYS CARDER
9 Inches High, 6 7/8 Inches Wide

Gladys, born in 1889, was Frederick Carder's daughter who married Gillett Welles. This plaque not only showcases Mr. Carder's skills as a sculptor, but is also a loving memory of his daughter as a young girl. In spite of being cast in a mold, this example is believed to be a family heirloom and may be the only such plaque

LUMINOR WITH MOLDED INTAGLIO CARVED BUST
OF THOMAS ALVA EDISON
10 9/16 Inches High, 8 1/2 Inches Wide

These luminors were presented to guests attending an October 21, 1929 banquet celebrating the opening of the Henry Ford Museum in Dearborn, Michigan. The subject of the plaque was Henry Ford's tribute to his friend, Thomas Alva Edison, commemorating the invention of the light bulb on its fiftieth anniversary.

IVORY PEAR TABLE DECORATION WITH LEAF ORNAMENT
6, 4 3/4, 3 3/4 Inches High
Shape #7474

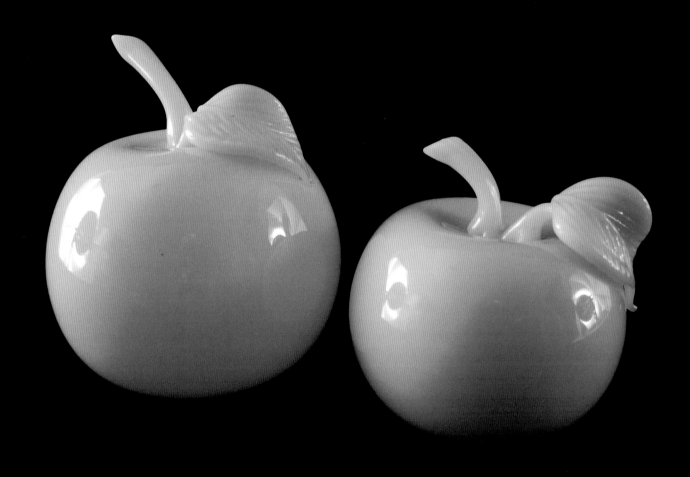

IVORY APPLE TABLE DECORATION WITH LEAF ORNAMENT
3 1/2, 3 Inches High
Shape #7474

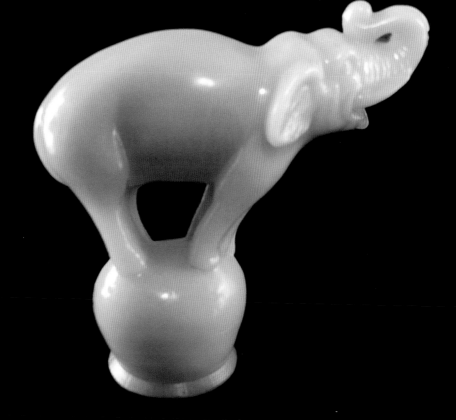

IVORY ELEPHANT
5 3/4 Inches High
Shape #7231

The Pierce Arrow automobile, which was manufactured in Buffalo, New York, offered this elephant decoration as an optional extra hood ornament.

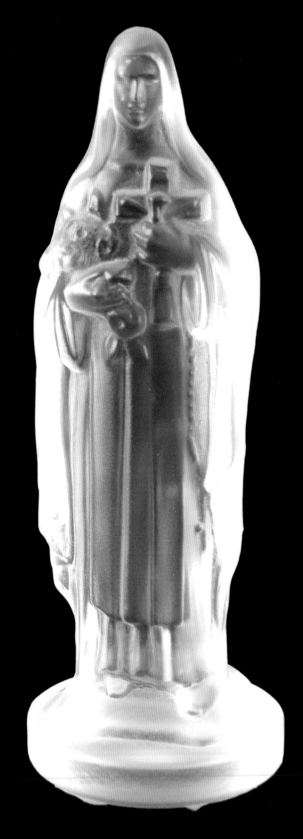

CLEAR CRYSTAL ST. THERESA LUMINOR WITH BLACK GLASS BASE
5 7/8 Inches High
8 1/8 Inches High with Glass Stand
Shape #7720

CRYSTAL FLOWER BLOCK WITH FEMALE FIGURE
8 1/2 Inches High
Shape #7039

CLEAR CRYSTAL FISH-SHAPED CONTEMPORARY ANGEL FISH

10 1/2 Inches High

Shape #7698

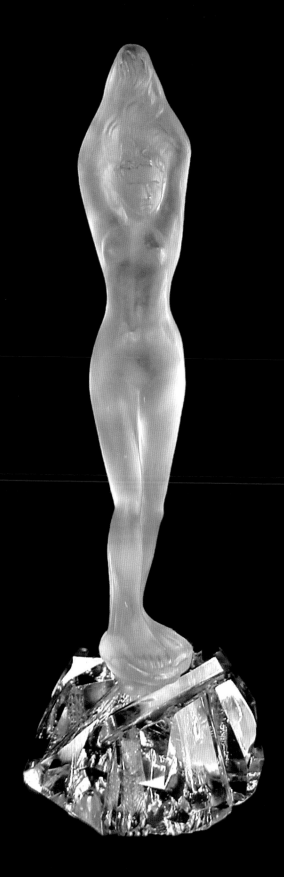

FROSTED BLUE DIVING GIRL IN MOONLIGHT ICEBERG FLOWER BLOCK
15 Inches High
Shape #6483

POMONA GREEN DOUBLE FISH IN DOUBLE TIERED FLOWER BLOCK
7 1/2 Inches High
Shape #7064
Flower Block #3269

CLEAR CRYSTAL PHEASANT
12 Inches Beak to Tail
Shape #6504
PRESSED AND CUT LEAD GLASS

BRILLIANT CUT GLASS FIGURES

These figures are formed in a mold and the feathers and other details added by the glass cutters after the pieces were annealed. Mr. Carder's figures are unconventional with bold cutting and textured backgrounds.

CLEAR CRYSTAL PIGEON
6 Inches High
Shape #6824
PRESSED AND CUT LEAD GLASS

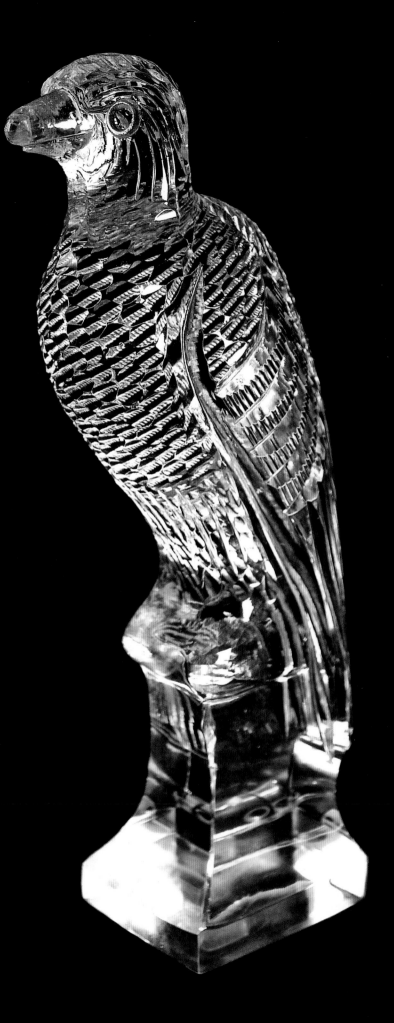

CLEAR CRYSTAL EAGLE

8 Inches High
Shape #6502
PRESSED AND CUT LEAD GLASS

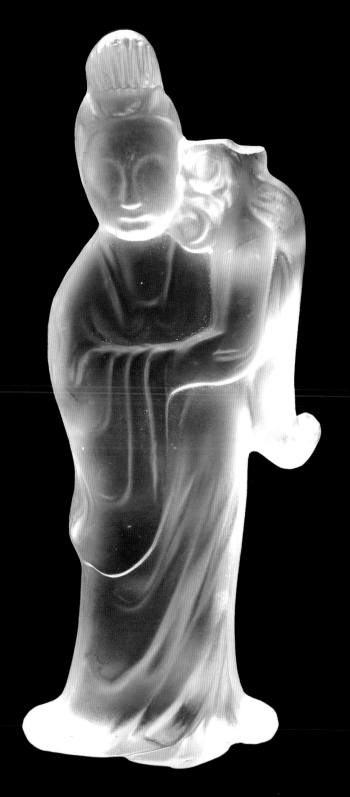

QUAN YEN FROSTED FIGURE
8 Inches High
Shape #7133

SOLID BALL LUMINOR WITH CONTROLLED BUBBLES ON HEAVY BRASS BASE
9 1/2 Inches High
Shape #6821

Decorative Arts

Art Glass, furniture, textiles, jewelry, ceramics, metal and architecture all embrace the Decorative Arts. They were designed and made to decorate our homes. I originally began collecting black amethyst pressed glass and the bold color of the black glass created a striking effect in our home.

When I discovered Mr. Carder's Steuben, I graduated to the next level. I found that Mr. Carder's classic training consistently delivered just the right form; the right balance of shape. While Mr. Carder did produce some black glass, he more importantly used black as an accent color, as a contrast to his other brilliant colors. The graduation process for me continued with other bold and dramatic colors. No glassmaker before or after had conquered such a bold color palette of over 140 colors. Mr. Carder wasn't satisfied with just the right shape and color, or the unique color combination that best complemented that shape, but he was always challenging himself with rediscovering the solution to some mystery of glass construction developed by the Romans, the Greeks, the Chinese or some other culture of ancient times. The measure of his inventiveness was his continual challenge to create some new combination or technique.

The changing taste of the public for Art Nouveau, Arts and Crafts, Art Deco, Venetian and Victorian spanned his productive years. He was undaunted and uniquely conquered every style, and mastered the times. From Steuben Glass Works, founded in 1903, and for the following thirty years, Mr. Carder created the tradition of excellence which has been sustained by America's greatest glass company more than 100 years after its founding. All of this suggests to me that Mr. Carder may, for all of these things, be the

greatest glassmaker of all times. Mr. Carder's name was not as well known as some of his contemporary art glassmakers, such as L.C. Tiffany or René Lalique, largely because his company didn't bear his name. However, arguably Mr. Carder was much more versatile, adaptable to the times and broadly accomplished than some better recognized names.

Art glass was intended to be used to decorate or for lighting the home. It was also many times intended to be used for more prosaic purposes, such as goblets and dinnerware. For this, I would suggest that collectors should feel duty bound to carry on this decorative tradition. This means utilizing these special Carder objects for home decor or lighting, as originally intended.

Only after I've decorated with as many Steuben objects as possible does the excess go into cabinets. I have included pictures from some of my custom cabinets designed for Mr. Carder's glass throughout this book. For cabinets, lighting is critical to properly show art glass. There is never enough. Standard furniture store cabinets with one or two halogens at the top, with deep shelves and mullions do not do justice to display. I use an abundance of halogens inside and outside my cabinets and narrow shelves that are only nine inches deep and without mullions which enable the viewer to get close to see the glass. It is, in my opinion, the only proper way to display these special works.

EPILOGUE

Color in nature can be a strong attractant. Nature will color a flower to draw bees that will pollinate a field or orchard. The very foods we eat whet our appetites with their brilliantly colored displays. Frederick Carder was consumed by color. In his thirty years at Steuben, about one hundred and forty colors were developed and named. This incredible profusion of color is in large measure what attracts so many people to the beauty of Steuben art glass.

Creating a color for glass was not done by calling a local supply house and ordering six tons of Celeste Blue. It was accomplished by adding chemicals, minerals, metals and even bone ash to the basic formula for lead crystal or soda glass. A formula had to be developed for each of the colors and each formula was strictly followed. Mr. Carder proved to be quite a chemist and his success with color became his success at Steuben.

Unfortunately, record keeping being what it was, combined with the absence of color film, today we can only match the names of about a third of those colors. The rest are lost to history and we will likely not unravel the mysteries of color at Steuben. That in no way diminishes our joy at adding a sunshine bright, Bristol Yellow bowl to our living room or a shocking splash of color to a corner with a Selenium Ruby vase. Steuben is not just glass, it is art. It captures our spirit and makes our hearts sing. We marvel at the color and the forms that make our homes and our lives more beautiful everyday.

RESOURCES

Gardner, Paul V., *The Glass of Frederick Carder,* New York: Atglen, PA. Schiffer Publishing Ltd., 1971

Thomas P. Dimitroff, *Frederick Carder and Steuben Glass: American Classics,* Atglen, PA, Schiffer Publishing Ltd., 1998

These texts are both in current publication and available at book stores. The Gardner text is the definitive work on the glass of Frederick Carder. All shape numbers referred to in this text may be found in Gardner's book where it republishes the Steuben factory line drawings.

The Dimitroff text is an important and essential enlargement upon the work of Gardner and an indispensable tool to the study of Frederick Carder glass.

A great learning tool and rich resource may be found at the website of The Carder Steuben Club at www.cardersteubenclub.com. This site also contains an extensive bibliography of resources.

Further, the world's most comprehensive collection of glass, which includes and displays the largest collection of Carder Steuben glass, is at the Corning Museum of Glass ("CMOG") in Corning, New York. The CMOG includes the extraordinary and extensive research facility of the Juliette K. & Leonard S. Rakow Research Library. See www.cmog.org.